Railway Herita

THE
NEWPORT DOCKS
& RAILWAY
COMPANY

ALEXANDRA (NEWPORT & SOUTH WALES) DOCKS
AND
RAILWAY COMPANY,
NEWPORT MON.

To my Dad, at Christmas 98
love from
Karen & Colin,
x

A GWR map of Newport Docks, edition of 1934. *Courtesy Mr D. C. Sims, Newport Harbour Commissioners Office*

RAILWAY HERITAGE

THE
NEWPORT DOCKS
& RAILWAY
COMPANY

A portrait of the Alexandra (Newport & South Wales) Docks & Railway, and the Pontypridd, Caerphilly & Newport Railway

John Hutton

Silver Link Publishing Ltd

I dedicate this book to my mother, Mrs N. L. Hutton,
and to the memory of my late father, Mr J. E. Hutton.

© John Hutton 1996

First published in October 1996

British Library Cataloguing in Publication Data

A catalogue record for this book is available from the British Library

ISBN 1 85794 087 3

Silver Link Publishing Ltd
Unit 5
Home Farm Close
Church Street
Wadenhoe
Peterborough PE8 5TE
Tel (01832) 720440
Fax (01832) 720531
e-mail: pete@slinkp-p.demon.co.uk

Printed and bound in Great Britain

Certificate of Incorporation of the Alexandra (Newport) Dock Company Ltd.
Courtesy Newport Public Library

CONTENTS

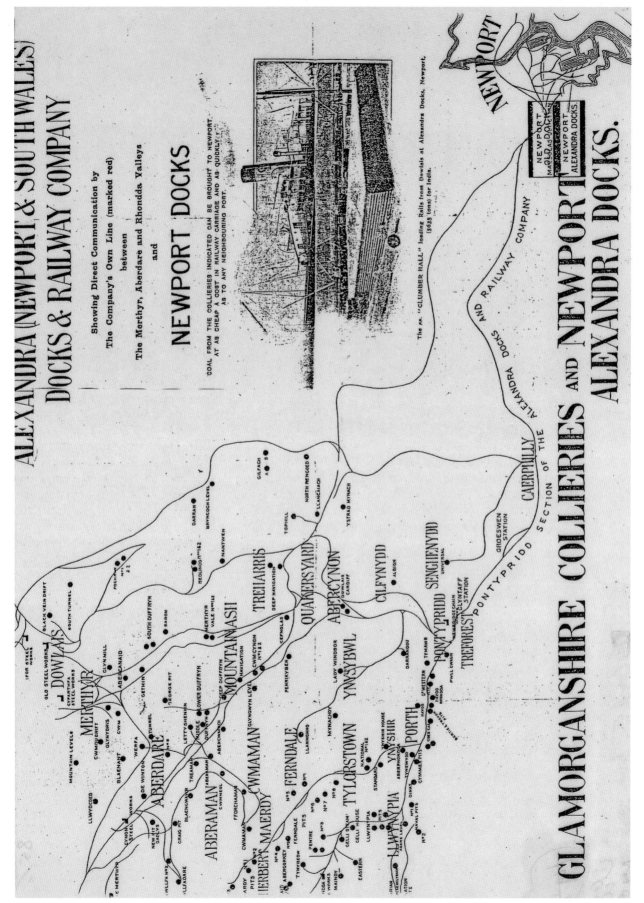

An ANDR Company map of the Glamorganshire Collieries and the PC&N line to Newport, November 1907. *Courtesy Cardiff Public Library*

INTRODUCTION

The Alexandra Docks at Newport was the brainchild of a group of influential businessmen who realised that the Old Town Docks there were fast becoming congested with the increase in water and inland traffic. On the instigation of the First Lord Tredegar, a movement was started towards the building of separate and larger docks. Eventually, after many months of negotiation, the Alexandra (Newport) Dock Company was born, incorporated by an Act of Parliament on 6 July 1865. The name Alexandra was taken from the marriage of His Royal Highness the Prince of Wales (later to become King Edward VII) to Her Royal Highness Princess Alexandra of Denmark in 1863.

Almost immediately work went ahead to excavate the area that would be known as the North Docks. Due to financial problems, however, this work did not go as quickly as had been planned, so it was not until 10 April 1875 that the North Dock and Lock was officially opened. In its first year the total imports and exports handled amounted to a total of 296,927 tons. By 1881 this total was 2½ million tons.

By the Act of Parliament of 1882 taking effect on 18 August, the two dock companies, the Alexandra (Newport) Dock Company and the Newport Dock Company, were amalgamated to become the Alexandra (Newport & South Wales) Docks & Railway Company (ANDR). On 1 January 1884 the ANDR also took over control of the Old Town Docks.

To tap into the rich coalfields of the Rhondda and Cynnon Valleys and bring the coal to the Alexandra Docks, the Second Lord Tredegar, along with other members of the board, decided to construct and finance a railway line that would start at the market town of Pontypridd, via a junction with the Taff Vale Railway Company station there. This would then head westwards to Caerphilly, and from there it would eventually reach the Alexandra Docks, the idea being to divert part of the tremendous amount of coal and iron traffic that otherwise would have found its way to the coal staithes of the Marquis of Bute Docks at Cardiff.

This line, to be known as the Pontypridd, Caerphilly & Newport Railway Company (PC&N), was incorporated by an Act of Parliament on 8 August 1878, but it was to be many years before the line was completed and able to carry mineral traffic, and later still for the carrying of passengers. Built of double-line width, it crossed the River Taff at Pontypridd, then followed the Glamorganshire Canal for a short distance before heading westwards to join the Rhymney Railway at Penrhos Junction, using that company's line into Caerphilly station. After leaving Caerphilly the ANDR used the line of the Brecon & Merthyr Railway, running along that company's metals to Basseleg Junction. From there the ANDR used the Great Western Railway Company lines for a short distance before reaching Newport and its own line leading into the internal system of the Alexandra Docks. This rather complicated journey was made all the more interesting by the fact that most of the rolling-stock used by the ANDR was former GWR stock, while the engines were driven for a number of years by drivers of the Taff Vale Railway.

Covering a total distance of just over 23 miles from the town of Pontypridd to the docks at Newport, there were also extensive sidings in use along the line and numerous lines inside the Alexandra Dock complex, so it is no wonder that by 1922 there were over 100 miles of track in use.

On 25 March 1922 the Alexandra (Newport & South Wales) Docks & Railway Company was amalgamated into the Great Western Railway Docks department, passing into British Railways hands on nationalisation in 1948. In 1982 the docks became part of the Associated British Ports group, and today can be described as an all-purpose port; although they do still handle traditional cargoes, they also handle vehicles, general cargo, fruit, machinery and timber. Equipped to handle vessels of up to 40,000 tons deadweight in a combined water area of some 125 acres, it is indeed a modern port and an important part of the ABP operation.

I hope that this book will give all railway and maritime enthusiasts and historians a large, yet varied subject to read and enjoy.

ACKNOWLEDGEMENTS

To all those people that shared a moment of their time with me:

Those staff and management of the Associated British Ports Group of Newport and Cardiff that I have had the pleasure of meeting over many years, some still in office and some now retired: Mr R. C. F. Williams, Port Manager, Newport; Mr Haydon Jones, now retired, ABP, Newport; Mr Tony Williams, for his help, ABP, Newport; Mr Roy Burrows, also for his help, ABP, Newport; Mr Ray Stanbury, now retired, ABP, Cardiff; Mr Kevin Francis and Mr John Phelps, for their help, ABP, Cardiff.

I am also grateful to Mr Doug Jones of Associated British Ports, Cardiff, former Public Relations Officer, now also retired, for his help and the use of the *Syren and Shipping* magazine, edition of 1904, and for the use of the photographs and the information contained within, which over a period of time could be lost for ever.

I should also like to thank the following:

Aberdare Public Library and staff; Avon Anglia Publications, Weston Super Mare, and Mr G. Body.

Mrs E. Bartlett, Maesglas, Newport; Mr M. C. Bird, Whitchurch, Cardiff, for his help with the coloured postcards; Mr N. L. Browne, Surrey; Brown & Lennox Company, Pontypridd, especially to Mrs Griffiths, Personnel Manager.

Cardiff Public Library and staff, for permission to use photographs and information from their ANDR booklet of 1907; Mr R. M. Casserley, Berkhamsted; Mr Ray Caston, Newport, for his help and expertise on these docks; Mr T. D. Chapman, Radyr; Mr John Cornwall, Bristol.

Mr J. J. Davis, Torquay, Devon; Mr J. Dore Dennis, Westra.

Mr David Fletcher, Librarian, Bovington Tank Museum, Dorset.

Great Western Railway Museum, Swindon, especially to the Curator, Mr Tim Bryan; Great Western Railway Staff Association Club, Newport, to the staff and members; Great Western Society, Didcot.

Mr V. C. Hardacre, Cardiff; Mr Cliff Harris, Porth, Rhondda, for his help and notes on the PCN line and these docks; Mr F. T. Hornby, Surrey.

Mr James, Forge and Hammer public house, White Hart, Machen; Mr D. K. Jones, Mountain Ash; Dr Stuart Owen Jones, Curator, Welsh Industrial and Maritime Museum, Cardiff; Mr Tony Jukes, for the loan of his photographs and the GWR booklet of 1934.

Mr C. Leigh, editor of *Steam World*, for the use of his notes on the Barnum & Bailey coaches taken from *Model Railway Constructor*, October 1983; Lens of Sutton, Surrey; Locomotive Club of Great Britain.

Mr B. J. Miller, Barry, S Glam; Mr Barrie Morris, Merthyr Tydfil, for his help, and also to all members of the Great Western Railway Staff Association at Merthyr, especially to Mr Mel Davies.

Newport Borough Council; Newport Public Library and staff, especially to Mr C. Graves and Mrs S. Pugh, Librarian; Newport Resource Centre and staff.

Oakwood Press, Headington, Oxford; Ordnance Survey Department, Southampton; Mr Graham Oxlande, Tonyrefail, Rhondda.

Mrs Parsons, Mendalgief, Newport; *Pontypridd Observer* newspaper and staff; Pontypridd Public Library, especially to Mr Adrian Burton and Mrs Penny Pugh for their help during my research; Mr Alun Powell, Rhydyfelin, for his helpful knowledge and his friendship over the years, also to his good wife Val, for putting up with me; Mr D. Rees, Pontypridd.

The Railway Magazine, especially the Editor, for permission to use excerpts and photographs from Vol 32 (1913), Vol 38 (1916), Vol 43 (1918), Vol 50 (1922), Vol 59 (1926); Mr Sid Rickard, Bishopbriggs, Glasgow; Mr D. J. Rees, Ynysybwl.

Mr David Sims, for the loan of the ANDR booklets of 1904, 1914, 1916, and for the hospitality shown in the Newport Harbour Commissioners Office; South Glamorgan Libraries; Mr D. Spargo, Machen; Mr J. Stacey, Newport; Starling Press Publications, Risca.

Mr D. G. Thomas, London; Mr J. B. True, Oxford, owner of *Trojan*.

Westrail Enterprises, Westra; Mr Alun Wetheridge, Great Western Railway Staff Association, Newport; staff of the Welsh Industrial and Maritime Museum, Cardiff, especially Mr G. Hayward; Welsh Railway Research Circle members; Mr R. Wilding, Pontypridd; Mr I. L. Wright, Cambridge.

My gratitude also to the widow of the late Mr C. R. Clinker and the publishers Avon Anglia, who gave permission to use the notes from his register of closed halts and stations; to the memory of the late Mr T. B. Sands of Cardiff, and to the late Mr H. C. Casserley, of Berkhamsted, who did much to record on film the now vanished scenes of the South Wales railways; to Mr A. Merchant, for permission to include the sketch of White Hart Halt drawn by the late Mr W. Merchant; to His Honour Judge D. Watkin Powell, for his permission to use his late father's photographs of 1910, when he was Chief Draughtsman for the ANDR (these photographs are now on permanent loan to the WIMM, Cardiff; it is due to the foresight of this gentleman and others like him that such photographic records of the ANDR system have remained intact over the years); to the memory of the late Arthur Wallis of Newport, a very knowledgeable man; and lastly to the many railway enthusiasts who spend their time undertaking the task of restoration, the rebuilding of our past, so that the youngsters of today will find some interest and learning from their endeavours.

1.
THE NORTH DOCK

The North Lock (Act of 1865)

Immediately after the opening speeches were made on 10 April 1875, a button was pressed and the huge dock gates opened electronically. In that first year 982 vessels would pass through the lock, which was some 350 feet in length and 65 feet wide, with access gained via the River Usk. Trade through the lock steadily increased, so much that eventually a new entrance lock had to be opened in 1914. As a result trade in the docks via the North Lock gradually decreased, and in 1919 this access was closed and converted into a dry dock, known as Messrs C. H. Bailey's Dry Dock. By 1934 this dry dock was extended to 415 feet in length, and the lock entrance to 60 feet wide. Today the dry dock is under the ownership of the Bristol Channel Ship Repairs Limited; with a length of 454 feet and a width of 64 feet, and is the only dry dock in use in the docks today.

In 1872 the Newport Harbour Commissioners decided that an accurate detailed account of the wharves and development along the River Usk, from the river's mouth to the town bridge, should be recorded. It was therefore decided that a photographer should capture the scenes on glass-plate negatives; he chartered a vessel and, mooring at certain points along the river, took a series of photographs, some of which are reproduced here.

Many problems were encountered with the digging out of the North Lock, which were to occur again many years later with the South Dock excavations. On 1 September 1874 the monthly report from Mr Parkinson to the Board of Directors stated that Mr Abernethy would be exceeding the estimate for completion of the docks owing to the exceptional character of the ground upon which the branch railways were being formed, and due to the repeated slips of the embankment, a great portion of which had to be re-formed no fewer than 25 times.

A rare photograph taken in 1872 showing the excavation process taking place at North Dock, with two fixed derricks hard at work. *Newport Harbour Commissioners Office*

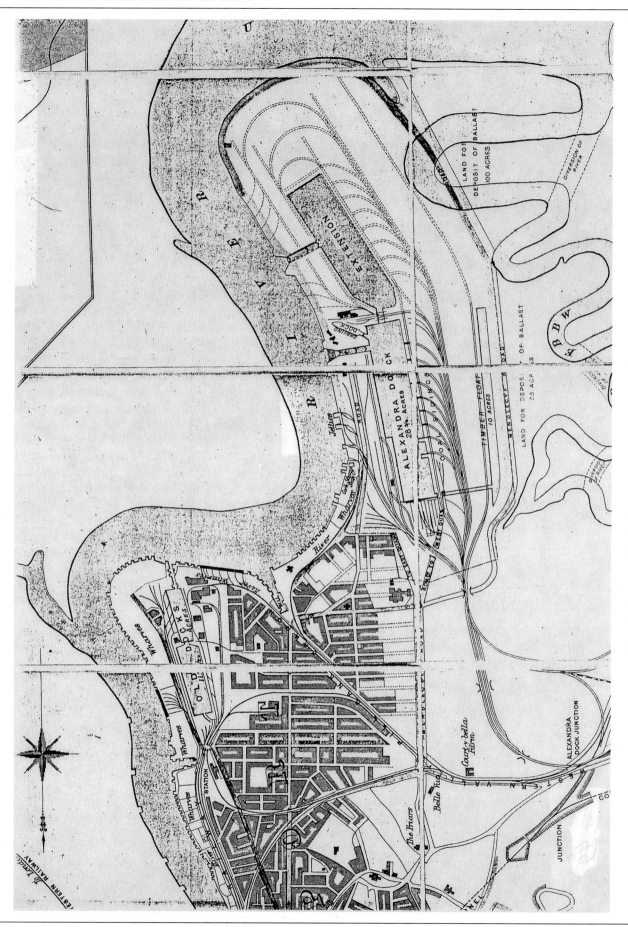

Map of the Alexandra Docks, Newport, circa 1884. *Cardiff Public Library*

This other photograph of 1872 shows the newly completed and erected lock gates of the North Lock entrance, with three steam cranes in view. Also on the left-hand side can be seen the new power station buildings that would supply the electric power to this lock. The buildings consisted of a pump and electrical generating house, economiser, water softening and feed pump house. *Newport Harbour Commissioners Office*

The North Dock (Act of 1865)

The North Dock opened for the handling of mineral and general traffic on the same day as the Lock, 10 April 1875. Immediately the opening ceremony was completed, a telegram was dispatched to His Royal Highness the Prince of Wales:

'The Mayor of Newport has the honour most respectfully to inform HRH the Prince of Wales that the Alexandra Dock, named after HRH the Princess of Wales, has been successfully opened in the presence of 40,000 people of all classes and amidst the universal rejoicings of the inhabitants of Wales.'

Within two hours the reply was received:

'The Prince of Wales, Sandringham, to the Mayor of Newport, Mon.
     I thank you very much for your telegram, and I congratulate most heartily the inhabitants of Wales on the success of the undertaking.'

During the excavation of the dock the remains of a Viking longship were discovered, lying at a depth of only 12 feet below the surface. Today the depth of water in the dock is 28 feet.

     Both the North and South Docks were electrically lit by 1904, this being very much an unprecedented move towards safety; gas was much cheaper but the most dangerous form of lighting in use at the time. Also at that time both docks were equipped with a total of 17 hydraulic coal hoists and 31 cranes of fixed and movable types, all operated by means of hydraulic pressure, created by steam power and ranging in pressure from 1½

tons per square inch to as much as 40 tons per square inch.

     After the Grouping of 1922 and the subsequent taking over of the docks by the GWR, improvements were made in all aspects; by 1932 they containing a total of 12 hydraulically operated cranes with a 30-ton lifting capacity, 18 hydraulic cranes with a 6-ton lift, 27 electric cranes also with a 6-ton lift, and nine steam cranes with a lifting capacity of 10 tons.

East Quay (later renamed as North Quay)

This quay was the location of the hydraulic cranes numbers 10, 12, 13 and 16 (which were of the movable type, with fixed jib and a lifting capacity of 3 tons), 11, 14 and 15 (movable type with fixed jib but with a lifting capacity of 6 tons), 17 (as 11, 14 and 15 but with a lifting capacity of 30 tons), 18 (fixed type with a fixed jib and a lifting capacity of 2½ tons) and 19 (fixed, with a fixed jib and a lifting capacity of 2 tons). By 1932 the GWR had installed a further eight hydraulic cranes on the East Quay, making a total of 18.

     Today this quay handles scrap metal and some coal imports. It is also used for the berthing of tugs. The No 2 warehouse situated on the quay handles cargo trade to the Continent.

GWR Macaw B-type bogie bolster, No 107027, carrying steel girders and photographed in March 1927 on the 70-ton weighbridge that was located at the East Quay side. On the extreme right can be seen a GWR ventilated van and an ANDR open wagon next to No 1 Transit Shed, North Dock.

     The extensive railway sidings that once ran along this side of North Dock have now been removed, leaving only a few lines for rail traffic, leading mainly to the No 2 warehouse and the South Docks area. *Associated British Ports*

The steamship *Ethelburga* discharging iron ore at the North Dock circa 1900. The photograph also shows some of the 16 hydraulic cranes in use at the time. Three types of lettering are known to have been used on the ANDR open plank wagons, and this view shows that most commonly used. The iron ore trade from these docks ceased in 1975 with the opening of the Port Talbot tidal harbour. *South Glamorgan Libraries*

A washer made to fit the dock's 100-ton crane photographed by the official docks photographer, whose task was to record every scene for posterity, on 14 July 1908. *Associated British Ports*

East Quay, North Dock, showing colliery pit-props being stacked and loaded on to Great Western Railway open wagons, en route to the collieries of the Western Valleys, circa 1900. The sailing ships in this photograph are three-masted barques, ideally suited for the carrying of cargoes such as timber or cotton. *ANDR booklet of 1916*

This close-up of the storage area for general cargo at East Quay on 4 June 1910 gives a good idea of the varied selection of traffic in use or waiting to be moved from the North Dock. The various wagons and vans consist of mainly tarpaulined four-wheel wagons; the one on the right, numbered 36500, is one of the GWR seven-plank type, while that numbered 43548 looks like a GWR five-plank. A selection of GWR box vans can also be seen, beyond which is what looks like one of the converted ANDR transit vans, and one of the newly acquired Barnum & Bailey coaches.

In the background is the Transporter Bridge, Newport's most famous landmark; the row of houses leading towards it is Watch House Parade. *Associated British Ports*

The SS *City of Khios* at berth at East Quay, with railway coaches for the Egyptian State Railways being shipped aboard via 30-ton crane No 17 circa 1910. This vessel was one of the Ellerman Line ships that provided a monthly service from Newport to the ports of Aden, Sudan, Mombasa and other East African ports. *ANDR booklet of 1916*

In about 1917 railway equipment is awaiting shipment to France for use by the War Department during the First World War. The Alexandra Docks handled a tremendous amount of war traffic during the war years, with the Salvage Factory girls working non-stop for the war effort. *Associated British Ports*

ANDR road vehicle No 4 being loaded with potatoes, helped by volunteers during the General Strike of 1926. Those solid tyres must have provided the driver with a bumpy ride! *Associated British Ports*

This 1936 photograph shows the SS *Rushpool* discharging iron ore, her first cargo for Ebbw Vale foundries, into 20-ton iron ore hoppers. This ship, with a Gross Registered Tonnage of 5,125, was built in 1928 but torpedoed by a German submarine while crossing the North Atlantic in January 1941. *Associated British Ports*

Timber Stage, East Side

Located on the east side of North Dock was the Timber Stage, 960 feet long and equipped with nine hydraulic cranes, and a quay wall, 1,160 feet long and equipped in 1914 with ten cranes, one of which could deal with loads of up to 30 tons. Also on the east side in 1914 were two large warehouses built for housing general imports.

The cranes situated on the Timber Stage were Nos 1, 2 and 3, with a lifting capacity of 2 tons, and Nos 4 to 8, which were the movable type and had a lifting capacity of 2½ tons. All these cranes had fixed jibs, as did No 9, which had a lifting capacity of 3 tons.

With the amalgamation of the Alexandra Docks into the GWR system in 1922, a considerable amount of money was spent on modernising and improving both North and South Docks.

This modernisation included a complete reconstruction of the Timber Stage in reinforced concrete, additional storage sidings for loaded and empty railway wagons, the adoption of coaling appliances for the emptying of 20-ton coal wagons, and the replacement of hydraulically operated cranes with the newer electrically operated luffing cranes. By 1934 the GWR had also provided additional sidings next to the Timber Stage for the handling and storage of general cargo traffic.

Today the north end of the dock is available for industrial development.

Poles and pit props being unloaded from the Swedish vessel *Tom of Landskrona* at the Timber Stage in May 1928. *Associated British Ports*

This 26 January 1927 view, again of the Timber Stage, gives quite a clear picture of the cranes purchased from Messrs Armstrong Whitworth Company in 1906. Also in view is engine No 676, originally Alexandra Docks No 3; it was withdrawn by the GWR in 1929, scarcely two years after this picture was taken. *Associated British Ports*

Above This busy scene was taken from near the ANDR Dock Company offices in September 1926, looking northwards in the direction of Watch House Parade. On the left are the cranes at the former East Quay, by then known as North Quay, with various open-type wagons in view belonging to the London, Midland & Scottish Railway and the pre-Grouping Great Eastern, Great Western and North Eastern companies. The steel hoppers are from the Blaenavon Big Pit Colliery. In front of the camera are GWR bolster wagons with loads of telegraph poles awaiting transporta-

tion, while on the right are GWR open six-plank wagons. Two have tarpaulin sheet rails fitted, while the remainder may be part of a common user wagon pool rather than being restricted to the GWR system. It looks as though some of them have transported animal feeds to the docks, judging by the amount of hay left in them. *Associated British Ports*

Below This photograph was taken a little further north, also about 1926 and also facing towards Newport town. On the extreme left can be seen the Timber Stage at the north end of North Dock (with the inevitable timber stacked up to over 30 feet high), and the road leading towards the dock gates, with what appears to be one of the dock's 1½-ton road vehicles. The sidings in front of the camera are quite congested with LMS and GWR open wagons loaded with sorted planks of various thickness, the bolster wagons carrying the heavier planks.

On the right there seem to be a lot of internal-user-only wagons. Also on the right are empty GWR bolster bogie wagons, and next to them Private Owner colliery wagons from the United National Collieries, and a group from the Black Vein Collieries, Risca.

On the extreme right are the coaling hoists of the ANDR-built River Wharf. The large building in the right background is the Mersey Insulation Company's works. In the far distance one of the ANDR shunting engines is about to pick up some of the empty wagons. All in all, a very busy scene indeed! *Associated British Ports*

ANDR engine No 19, an 0-6-0 saddle tank, at work around the North Dock on 31 July 1905, hence the use of spare chains and oil cans. One of the ANDR two-plank open wagons can also be seen, possibly on shunting duties. No 19 was built by Messrs Peckett in 1886, renumbered by the GWR as 680, and eventually scrapped in 1948. *LCGB (Ken Nunn Collection)*

West Side

The coaling hoists of the North Dock were located on the west side, and by 1914 consisted of three movable hoists. These were numbered by the ANDR as Nos 1, 2 and 7; Nos 1 and 2 had a lift of 48 feet above coping level, and No 7 a lift of 28 ft 9 in. In addition to these movable hoists there were six hoists of the fixed type, numbered 3, 4, 5 and 6; Nos 3 and 5 had a lift above coping level of 46 feet, Nos 4 and 6 only 28 ft 6 in. The other two hoists on this side were lettered A and B and were situated on projecting jetties, having a lift of 27 ft 9 in. These coaling hoists were operated hydraulically and had three lines of rails leading to them from the Marshalling Sidings situated further over to the west.

In the *GWR Magazine* of 1932 a short article appeared with reference to the North Docks:

'Newport. A new movable hoist having a lifting capacity above water level of 66 feet, with low and high level traversers for loaded and empty wagons, respectively, and capable of dealing with 20 ton wagons, had been erected in substitution of number 6 hoist, North dock, thus the company completes a pledge given to the people of Newport, that when the powers were obtained by the Company's Act of 1929 to close the Old Town Dock, the company then agreed with the corporation to remove two hoists from the Town Dock to the Alexandra Dock, and erect a movable hoist at the latter dock.'

The article also stated that five new 3-ton electric cranes had been provided on the South Quay side of the South Docks.

All the coal hoists and the extensive sidings had been finally removed by the 1960s, and today only the jetties of A and B remain. Too costly to remove, they serve as a reminder of busier times. This area is now the main stacking area for the storage of timber, under the guidance and supervision of Messrs Meyer South & West Limited.

By 1906 the coal and fuel exports handled from the Alexandra Docks amounted to 5,104,990 tons, an increase of 973,320 tons since 1896 (4,131,670 tons), and was to rise to over 6 million tons by 1914. This photograph shows the loading of coal aboard a vessel in North Dock circa 1900. In the background can be seen the tall masts of wooden sailing ships, still a common sight even at this late period of shipping technology. *South Glamorgan Libraries*

Left Movable hoists on the west side of North Dock, circa 1900; the one nearest the camera is No 2. *Associated British Ports*

Above One of the fixed hoists, in this case No 5, circa 1917. Beyond can be seen the viaducts, or 'roads' as they were known, from Nos 6, 7 and 8 hoists, which led the empty wagons back to the storage sidings. *Associated British Ports*

Open-type colliery wagons from the Tir Pentwys Black Vein Colliery Company, in this case carrying coal from the Tir Pentwys Colliery at Pontypool, at the No 5 hoist at North Dock circa 1904. *Syren and Shipping magazine*

A Partridge, Jones & Company advertisement from the ANDR booklet of 1914.
Associated British Ports

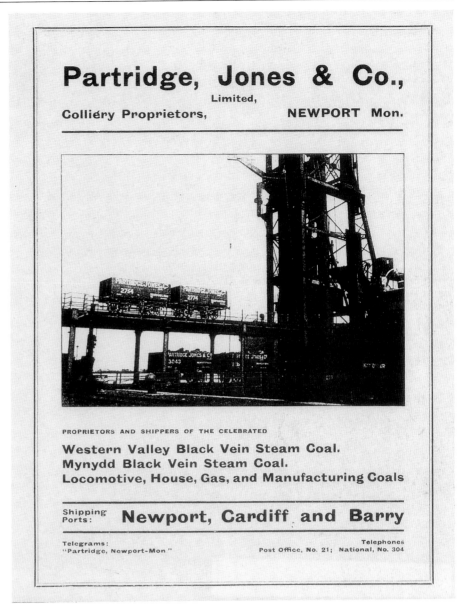

Colliery wagons of Partridge, Jones & Company of Abersychen, circa 1900, in this case belonging to the Blaensychen Colliery. *South Glamorgan Libraries*

Colliery wagons of the Powell Duffryn Steam Coal Company of New Tredegar, belonging to the East & West Elliot Pits, New Tredegar, circa 1900. *South Glamorgan Libraries*

Coal awaiting shipment, in wagons belonging to the Albion Black Vein Colliery and the John Blundell Black Vein Colliery of Pontypool (left), and in six-plank open wagons of Bailey & Roberts (right), circa 1900. *South Glamorgan Libraries*

Private Owner wagons of the United National Colliery Company carrying coal from the Black Vein Colliery, Risca, circa 1900. *South Glamorgan Libraries*

Timber Float, West Side

The Timber Float, located on the west side of the North Dock, was opened in 1878; it ran parallel with the North Dock, and covered an area of some 10 acres, with a depth of 8 feet, being connected to the North Dock via a canal. All logs floated through this canal were counted and numbered individually. It is interesting that, when completed, the dock was filled with fresh water, not sea water, mainly at the wishes of the traders of Newport, who were to use the facilities of these docks.

Later, possibly in the 1930s, the GWR added another Timber Float, also running parallel and situated a short distance from the original ANDR float, this one covering an area of 5¼ acres.

Today the canal and timber floats have been filled in and the area is also a part of the extensive timber storage yard used by Messrs Meyer East & West Limited.

The firm of Burt Bolton & Hayward is also located at the west side of the docks. This long-established business deals with the storage and handling, as well as the creosote treatment, of all forms of timber from telegraph poles to planed planks. It occupies the site of the former Messrs Batchelors works, a family firm that was established in 1812. This photograph shows wood being off-loaded at the west side of North Dock circa 1900, most of it being pitwood from Scandinavia and North America, en route to the collieries of the Rhondda and Western Valleys. *South Glamorgan Libraries*

The River Wharf

The River Wharf was located on the west bank of the River Usk, adjoining the entrance to the Alexandra North Dock. It had quayage of 403 feet, and was equipped with four movable cranes, Nos 28, 29, 30 and 31, all with a fixed jib and a lifting capacity of 2 tons.

Plans for the building of this wharf were drawn up by the end of 1904, with the work starting in 1905. It was renamed by the GWR as the GWR Wharf and closed just prior to the start of the Second World War, but was re-opened for the handling and shipping of coal to the Bristol and Avonmouth Docks. It even handled to a limited degree some coal exports to the Continent.

River Wharf, sometimes called Riverside Wharf, under construction in November 1905. This photograph gives a good idea on the use of the steel pile-drivers; as can be seen this one is poised ready to be driven downwards. This action was repeated time and time again until a sufficiently deep hole was made to take the main supports of the jetty. In the background can be seen the Transporter Bridge, also under construction, with scaffolding in evidence at the top of the western tower. *Associated British Ports*

Above Another view of River Wharf under construction in October 1905. *Associated British Ports*

Below River Wharf with the navvies, gangers and contractors, including dog, posing upon what appears to be the finished job, circa 1906. The Transporter Bridge was also opened on 12 September of that year. *Associated British Ports*

This excellent photograph gives a good indication of the layout of and activity within the docks circa 1922. In the foreground are the various jetties of the River Wharf area jutting out into the River Usk, some of the privately owned ones by now in a state of neglect, possibly as a result of the decline of the coal trade.

Beyond the jetties on the extreme left-hand side of the photograph can be seen the North Lock and the entrance into North Dock; although it still contains water, the lock was out of use by this time. A short distance to the right can be seen No 2 shed, then over on the west side the vast area of sidings and coal hoists, behind which can just be seen the Timber Float.

Stretching away into the distance is the River Ebbw, and joining North Dock to South Dock is Junction Cut with its swingbridge in the closed position. Beyond is South Dock, with the coal hoists on its west side marking its boundary. *Courtesy John Cornwall*

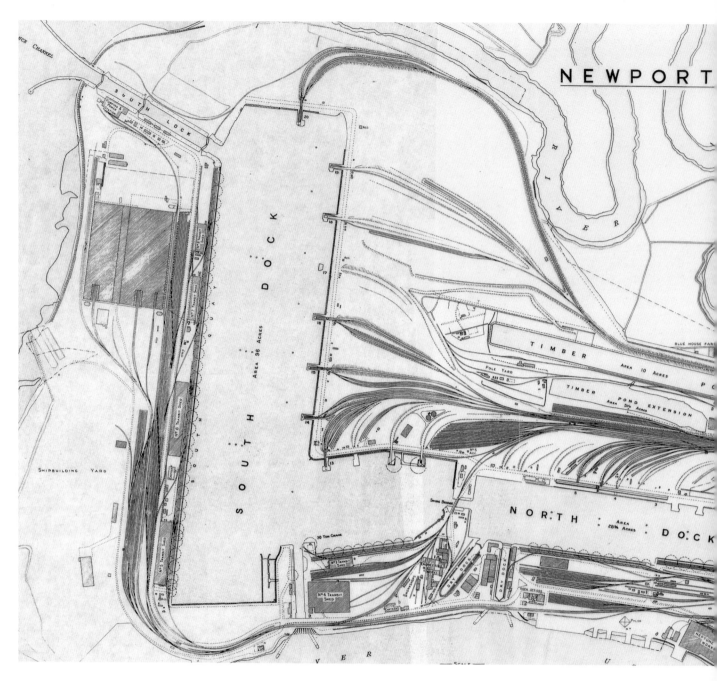

British Transport Commission map of the Alexandra Docks, circa 1950. In the top right-hand corner is Park Junction, and the PC&N connection from there to West Mendalgief Junction, just across the South Wales main line, is shown as lifted. At the junc-

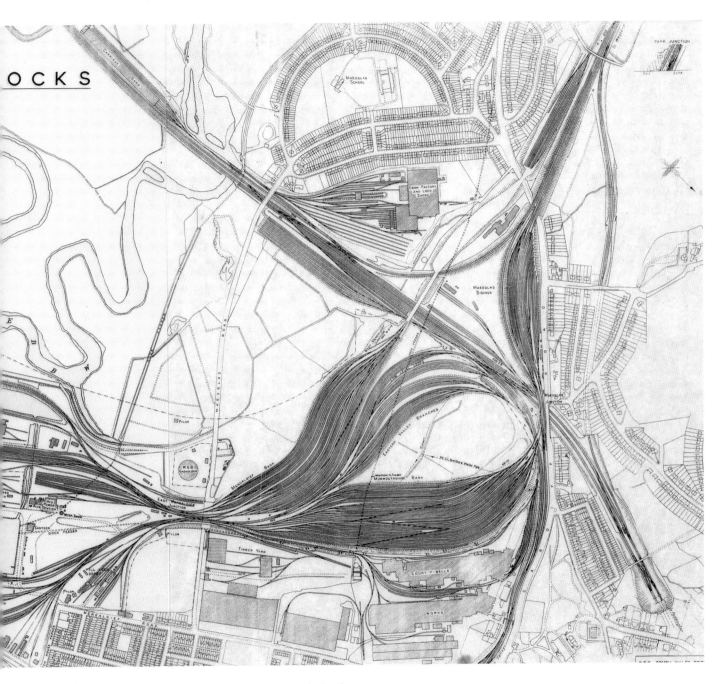

tion of the sidings complex and the entrance to North Dock is Mendalgief East Junction. Maesglas Junction is north of West Mendalgief, above Alexandra Dock Junction on the South Wales main line. *Associated British Ports*

Alexandra Graving Dock
(entered from the North Dock)

This Graving Dock was situated at the south-east corner of the North Dock, and measured 532 feet in length from the gates to the head of the dock, the width of the entrance being 50 feet, and the dock width 74 feet. Today no trace is left of it, as it has been completely filled in.

Dry docks

Alexandra Docks contained a Commercial Dry Dock with an entrance from the North Dock. It was 523 feet long and 74 feet wide; the entrance measured 49 ft 11 ins wide, which became 50 feet with the removal of the batter (inward inclination) on the entrance walls in 1934, the depth of water remaining at 20 feet to the outer sills. The ship repairs in this dock were carried out by whoever the ship-owner selected. The Commercial Dry Dock was filled in by 1958.

In addition, there were six private dry docks located nearby, with entrances from the River Usk; the largest, that of the Cardiff Channel Dry Dock & Pontoon Company Limited, was 785 feet long, with an entrance 65 feet wide. Others were the Eastern Dry Dock, measuring 360 feet long and 57 feet wide, later lengthened to 430 feet, and by 1934 under the ownership of the Mountstuart Dry Dock Company; the Mary Dry Dock, 350 feet long and 60 feet wide; the Alice Dry Dock, 289 ft by 46 ft 6 ins; and the Edith Dry Dock, 220 feet by 36 feet. These four dry docks were owned by Messrs Mordey, Carney & Company Ltd. Finally there was the Tredegar Dry Dock, owned by the Tredegar Dry Dock & Wharf Company Ltd, which was 712 feet long with a width of 65

feet. By 1934 this dock had also passed into the ownership of Mountstuart.

North Dock Central Hydraulic Power Station

The Central Power Station provided the power to operate almost all of the facilities in the docks, including hoists, hydraulic cranes, lock gates, the Rolling Bridge, swingbridge, capstans, etc, and was situated at the north end of North Dock. It was of brick construction, consisting of the engine house, boiler house, pump house and economiser house. At the south end of this building stood the chimney stack, which rose to a height of 140 feet, and near the chimney were three storage and controlling accumulators.

Steam was supplied to the engines, of which there were four, at a pressure of 185 lbs per square inch, generated in a range of seven Lancaster boilers, to give a blow-off pressure of 200 lbs. The temperature of the water, obtained from the town's supply and also from the ANDR company's own fresh water supply, was raised from 40 degrees to 400 degrees Fahrenheit.

Subsequently this power station was converted into engineering shops, and today all traces of it have long gone.

Today's Alexandra Docks, under the ownership and guidance of Associated British Ports, have changed almost beyond belief from the original design and concept of Lord Tredegar, but one cannot help but feel that they have lived up to and perhaps surpassed the expectations of the ANDR General Manager, John Macauley, who was very much a man of vision. Although today the coal trade is not handled to the scale that it once was, there have been other developments that have replaced this trade.

The three-masted vessel *Celestial Empire* in the Commercial Dry Dock. Records show that this vessel was in dry dock from 31 July to 2 August 1906, docked stern first, with the barque *Edward Preeg*. *Associated British Ports*

2.
THE SOUTH DOCK

Junction Cut (Swingbridge Junction)

Junction Cut is situated between the North and South Docks, connecting them via a channel about 60 feet in width. It was spanned by a swingbridge 125 feet long, which connected the west side of North Dock with the east side of South Dock; the bridge was operated hydraulically, the machinery being supplied by Sir W. G. Armstrong Mitchell & Company Ltd. It was over this

Junction Cut, or Swingbridge Junction as it was also known, in about 1934 - Alexandra Dock divers are about to commence work on the deepening of the lock by the removal of the lock inverts. This photograph is also quite historic, as it records for the first time the use of pneumatic drills underwater. This was to be a trial run of great importance.

Left to right: linesman F. Kilby (later to become a diver himself); diver Joe Wallis (father of Arthur Wallis); Inspector Bert Gumbrill; unknown (a representative of the firm making the drills); diver Fred Lewis; and linesman Arthur Lewis. *Courtesy of the late Mr A. Wallis*

swingbridge that rail access was gained to the original engine shed of 1875.

Today this cut is little more than a channel between two docks, a little overgrown in places, with the land on either side providing plenty of cover for the nests of water-birds.

The South Lock (Act of 1882)

This was the original entrance to the South Dock; opened in 1893, it enabled vessels to reach the South Dock from the River Usk. It was built to a length of 503 ft 6 ins and a width of 72 feet, and maintained a water depth in the lock of 25 feet, rising to 35 feet during spring tides.

South Lock was renamed East Lock with the opening of the new South Lock in 1914, and was closed during the middle period of the First World War, possibly 1916, although it was still regarded as an emergency entrance to the docks for many years until finally being filled in during 1937.

Access for road and rail traffic to the South Quay of South Dock across the original South Lock was gained by crossing a roller bridge, built in 1909. Originally this bridge carried a double set of railway lines, set in the ground as was usual in industrial locations, and was also provided with an overhung footbridge for pedestrian use.

The travel of this bridge was 107 feet, and the whole structure was carried on brick piers with cast iron cylinders. Railway signals were located on either side of the gates that guarded the approaches to the bridge. The levers to operate the bridge were located in a signal cabin on the north side of the lock.

After the lines to the Salvage Factory were extended the bridge was fixed in position, the name changing to Rolling Bridge Junction in 1915.

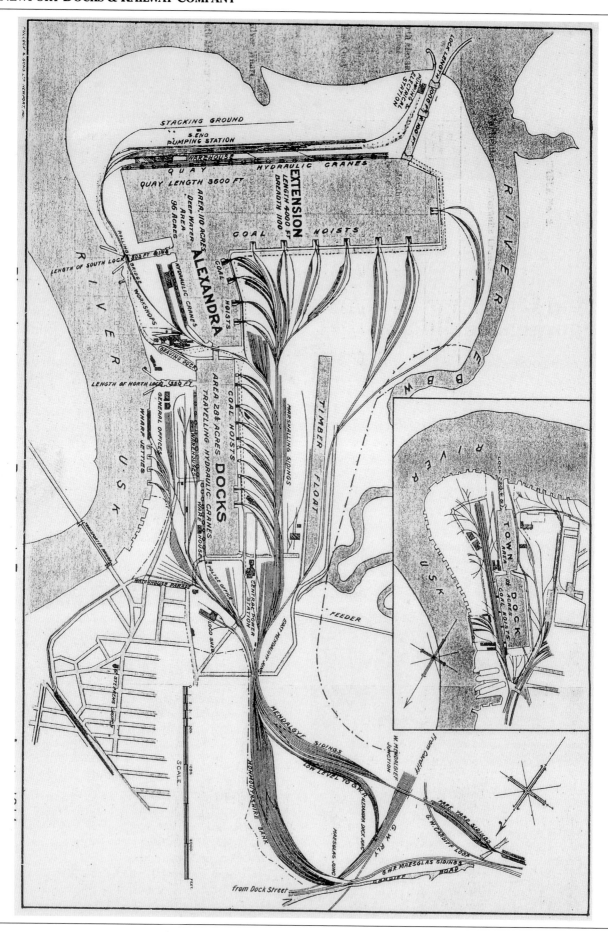

Left An ANDR map of April 1914 showing the North and South Docks and the South Dock Extension. *Courtesy Mr D. C. Sims*

Above An aerial view corresponding to the map opposite (the dark patches are the shadows of clouds). Taken in 1948, it gives a good view of the Timber Float on the right, while in the middle left can be seen the arms of the original North Lock entrance. Below that the riverside River Wharf coal hoists are still standing, although some of the runs leading to the coal hoists on the west side of North Dock have been taken up. Junction Cut can also be clearly seen joining the North and South Docks. In the top right-hand corner is South Lock. The blocks of houses in the bottom left-hand corner consist of Watch House Parade, Alexandra Road and Mendalgief Road, and to the right of them is the ANDR's Pill engine shed. *Associated British Ports*

Right The rolling bridge on 12 December 1908, during its construction. It was provided to carry road and rail traffic over the original South Lock for access to the South Dock Extension work. The signal box erected at Roller Bridge Crossing was there not only for the movement of railway traffic but also as an observation post to offset the likelihood of any accidents when the bridge was in the open position. *Associated British Ports*

The new South Lock (Act of 1906)

The new South Lock was also known as the Great Sea Lock, as the entrance was from the Bristol Channel and not the River Usk as in the older lock. Work was started by the contractors, Messrs Easton Gibb & Son, in December 1906, and the work took many years, the new lock not being completed until 1914.

On 14 July 1914 the lock was officially opened by HRH Prince Arthur of Connaught, son of King George V.

The lock has a total length of 1,000 feet and a width of 100 feet, being divided by watertight gates into two compartments of 600 and 400 feet respectively. Today it is the only entrance into the docks.

Notes in the Associated British Ports archive state that the first vessel into the South Dock via the newly opened South Lock was the steam yacht *Liberty*, built in 1908 and owned by Lord Tredegar; it broke a ribbon that had been placed across the lock entrance, and was then secured alongside the pump house.

After declaring the lock open, Prince Arthur and the dignitaries disembarked to inspect the pump house and staff before re-embarking to continue their passage into the South Dock.

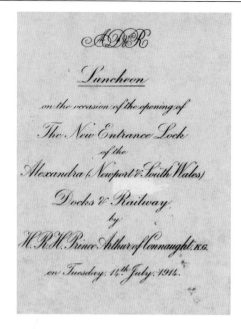

Above The luncheon invitation on the opening of the new South Lock, 14 July 1914. *Courtesy Newport Public Library*

Below The new South Lock under construction on 21 May 1908, with contractors' temporary lines and shoring timber much in evidence. Also in view is the river bed of the diverted River Ebbw. *Associated British Ports*

Above The view looking eastwards from the inner end of the new South Lock on 20 June 1908. The eastern section of the lock was opened in 1907. *Associated British Ports*

Below A close-up of the Manning Wardle contractor's engine seen in the previous photograph. On the right can be seen one of the contractor's steam cranes, with plenty of temporary track; although sharply curved and uneven, the heavy loads that this type of track withstood during this excavation work on these docks was quite remarkable. *Associated British Ports*

This photograph, dated 27 July 1908, was taken by the official Alexandra Dock photographer, employed to record the building and excavation of the South Lock and Dock. It shows two of the contractors posing next to one of the steel piles used for drilling the jetty foundations for the new South Lock entrance. These piles would be driven down under great pressure, hence the pointed end, specially made for this essential work. *Associated British Ports*

Contractors on the site of the new entrance jetties, 24 October 1908. The problems overcome by the type of soil encountered were numerous; described by them as liquid mud, it can quite easily be seen here clinging to the men, the dredging bucket and just about everything else in sight! *Associated British Ports*

The excavated site of the Middle Gates area of the new South Lock on 19 November 1909. Note the inevitable steam cranes and what appear to be metal-studded, possibly reinforced, contractors' wagons, all fitted with 'dumb buffers', ie wooden blocks. These wagons were made by the contractors themselves to carry the tremendous weight of the heavy soil. In the background can be seen one of the temporary water tanks, and to its right the rotary cement mixer.
Associated British Ports

The South Dock (Act of 1882) and South Dock Extension (Act of 1904)

The original length of the South Dock when opened on 6 June 1893 was 1,500 feet, with a width of 650 feet, thus covering an area of some 20 acres. The tonnage of vessels using the North Dock increased dramatically by no less than three-quarters of a million tons even while the new dock was being constructed. One advantage of the new South Dock was that the larger vessels entering the North Dock could now do so via the newly opened South Lock (later the East Lock), as the depth of water in this lock was the same as that of the North Dock.

However, after a while it was obvious that yet further expansion would be needed to handle the ever-increasing traffic, and by 1903 plans were put into operation to extend once again. The surveying work started in 1904, carried out by Mr Cuthbert and Mr Brereton MInstCE for the firm of Sir John Woolfe Barry & Partners, the resident ANDR engineer being Mr J. D. C. Couper.

The excavation work for the first part of the South Dock Extension was again contracted to Messrs Easton Gibb & Son of Westminster in May 1905, and they wasted no time. Work started in the June of that year to recover the 48 acres required.

In September 1907 the ANDR recorded: 'Situated between the South Dock (in the bank) and the first part of this extension (which was the former entrances to the timber float) piles were driven to secure the junction of this extension, with a formal agreement taking place that this would be the spot at which to make the sluice gate required to fill this extension with water from the existing dock, which would find its own way down into the newly excavated area of 48 acres. To effect this a portion of the piles were cut away to a depth of 10 feet and a large sluice gate was placed in that space, temporary piles having already been driven in.

'When the time was right, at a given moment these piles were lifted up by one of the travelling cranes; with the clay of the embankment having already been cut away and the stones removed, the way was clear. Steadily a trickle of water began its journey down this man-made chute, finding its own way to its destination. When the cutting of this bank had proceeded far enough, the sluice gate was again raised and the stream of water again began its flow into the newly extended dock. A total of between 400,000,000 and 450,000,000 gallons of water was required. This work took nearly a month before the correct levels were obtained, with the remainder of the water being pumped into one of the cut-off parts of the River Ebbw.'

The newly started excavation work on the new South Dock Extension in about 1904; it can be seen how the shape is being formed as layer after layer of soil is removed. Also in view is one of the contractor's engines with what looks like a full load. *Associated British Ports*

The bank referred to was dredged and the sludge pumped into another part of the disused area of the River Ebbw.

The ANDR booklet of 1914 stated that one of the most difficult undertakings of the extension work was the damming of the River Ebbw, which had to be undertaken at four different points at each end of the diversion, the aim being to close the old channel, and at the north and south sides of the dock respectively, to complete the quay that enclosed the extension.

A very clear description of the work undertaken by Easton Gibb & Son was outlined in the ANDR company booklet of 1906:

'Speaking generally, the level of the ground on the dock site was 6 to 7 feet lower than the level of the quay, and as the area was desired for siding accommodation it has all to be embanked to the latter level. A large proportion of the excavation has had to be taken out in the dry, for the formation of these extensive embankments means that the material has to be taken partly from that area of the extension lying to the east

One of the contractor's steam navvies is seen here at work circa 1908 beside one of the former farm buildings that was situated on the land before it was acquired for the dock extension. *Associated British Ports*

of the River Ebbw, and partly from the site of the river diversion.

'On the former site, the method used differed. The total depth of 39 feet has been tackled in three lifts of about 13 feet each with an occasional four lifts where the original ground level was somewhat higher. The excavated material is drawn from the bottom of the dock, up two inclines, one on the south and one of the north side of the extension, and this is then led to the spoil banks. No winding engines have been employed as the locomotive power is amply sufficient for the gradients in use.

'While making its first cut in any lift, the steam navvy is driven forward and downward, working in a "gullet", that is cutting on both sides. When the desired depth of lift has been obtained, the machine moves forward on the level, but still cutting on both sides. Upon the first cut being completed the steam navvy is drawn back, and again moves forward, cutting only one side and thus widening the gullet, and so on, until the first lift is complete over the required area.

'A somewhat different method was used for the removal of the quantity of material in the River Ebbw diversion, which it was necessary to excavate in the dry.

Here the shape of the cutting and its great length, as compared with its width, and the extreme flatness of the slopes, went against the use of what may be called the "incline and gullet" system. Accordingly a bucket land dredger of the 'Lubecker' type was brought into use. This machine, by the manipulation of its ladder, is able to cut the slope to any required angle, or incline, and has the further advantage of excavating to a considerable depth, below the level of the rails on which it stands, thus avoiding the necessity of using gradients as in the case of the steam navvies.

'For the conveyance of excavated material from the cutting, the Lubecker machine is self-propelling, and while working passes slowly over a stationary train of wagons, delivering into these the contents of its bucket. The ladder carrying the buckets works over the side instead of fore and aft, as in a floating dredger. The top lift of the diversion to a depth of 14 feet has been completed by this machine in a series of parallel cuts, the flood bank at either end being left intact to prevent the ingress of water. The quantity still to be removed from the diversion will be taken out by sea dredger, which has already made considerable progress with this work.

Many thousands of tons of wood were needed for shoring up the excavations during the construction of the South Dock Extension. This photograph gives an idea of how stout the timbers had to be to be able to withstand the tremendous pressure that was applied to the cross-bracings of the excavation trenches. Photographed on 24 August 1908. *Associated British Ports*

Above It was on the east side near this location that the first engine shed, built in 1875, was situated. By 1890 this two-road shed, quoted as being 123 ft 6 ins long by 33 feet wide, was insufficient to house and cope with the increased locomotive work needed by the contractors working on the South Dock Extension, so in 1904 the contractors built their own shed to house their Manning Wardle engines. The newly built shed, made of corrugated tin sheeting and with a temporary water tank nearby, is seen here. *Associated British Ports*

Left This slightly different view of the same location shows one of the contractor's Manning Wardle engines circa 1904. A total of five were used by Messrs Easton Gibb & Son during the excavation work. *Associated British Ports*

'The part of the extension laying between the west bank of the River Ebbw and the site of the diversion has been taken out to the full depth by means of dredging, the river being tidal with a range of 34 feet at spring tides and 15 feet at neap tides. The dredging was necessarily intermittent, with no work being possible at low water.'

Many problems were faced during these excavations. Because of the tidal flow of the River Ebbw, work had to be done by day and night; this cut a normal four-year contract down to around two years, but because artificial lighting was used the normal risks involved with excavation and shunting were increased threefold. Other difficulties were also met and overcome - even the soil was treacherous, as it was of an alluvial deposit known as 'bungham', which needed only the briefest spell of rain to convert it into a liquid mud. Eventually upwards of 3,600,000 tons of this deposit was excavated.

This bungham deposit also had a very adhesive quality, which caused the service roads to sink, even though as many as three or four layers of close timbers had been sunk to provide a suitable foundation. Even the angle of the banks could only be achieved at an angle of not more than four to one, and that 'with difficulty'.

The dry excavation work was undertaken by Messrs Ruston, Proctor & Company, with the use of their steam navvy of the Lubecker bucket type, already referred to. A costly but powerful machine, of which it was the only example in the country, it saved many, many hours of manual labour.

The removal of the excavated material to the spoil banks was accomplished by the use of a small army of locomotives owned by Messrs Manning Wardle & Company, as well as the use of several hundred side-tip wagons, specially built by the contractors themselves and of a size larger than previously used in public works. For the excavation in the 'wet' a large sea dredger, three powerful tugs and a number of dumb hopper barges of 500-ton capacity worked day and night, a tremendous achievement.

With the 48 acres added, this Extension was opened in November 1907; finally a further 27 acres was added, which was opened, along with the South Lock, on 14 July 1914. This brought the total area covered by land to 110 acres and a total water surface of 96 acres, with a depth of

33 feet; later this was dredged to 38 feet. During 1906 two coal hoists were built for the Extension, each being capable of handling loaded coal wagons with a gross weight of 23 tons. These were supplemented by another two hoists in 1908.

After the Grouping of the railways and docks during the 1922 to 1923 period, the Alexandra (Newport & South Wales) Docks & Railway Company became known as the Great Western Railway's Newport Docks. By 1934 they had a total of 27 electrically operated cranes, and 12 that were hydraulically operated, with the length of the completed South Dock being 4,000 feet, and 1,000 feet wide.

In 1908 the siding accommodation on the north side of South Dock, including goods sheds, covered an area of 600,000 square yards, with a total amount of track within the Alexandra Docks complex of over 100 miles. By 1932 the South Dock had seven transit sheds, which covered a floor area of 708,855 square feet. These sheds contained the various commodities, including grain, flour, general merchandise and even building sand, to name but a few, that were handled by the docks before the Second World War.

This photograph, taken on 1 September 1910 and looking northwards towards the inner gates on the east side, shows in the background the finished 12-foot diameter delivery culvert in place in the east side of the South Lock walls. This culvert will carry water from the River Usk through into the new South Dock, impounding 10 million gallons of water per hour. *Associated British Ports*

South Dock from the air in about 1935 - this photograph, taken from the southern point of the completed South Dock facing south-east, shows on the left the coaling hoists on the West Quay, with hoist No 19 nearest the camera and No 14 furthest away. At the top left-hand corner is the East Lock and No 4 transit shed at the East Quay. On the right are vessels at berth at South Quay. The foremost vessel is berthed next to the No 7 transit shed, with No 6 transit shed in the middle of the quay. The River Usk can be seen in the distance. The three ships moored together at the bottom of this photograph are situated next to No 20 coal hoist. *Associated British Ports*

South Quay

Built by Messrs Easton Gibb & Son during the extension work of the South Dock, the South Quay consisted of a concrete wall some 3,600 feet long, which by 1914 was equipped with 20 hydraulic cranes having a varied lifting capacity of between 1½ and 10 tons. The length of the quay was sufficient in length to berth nine vessels of an average of 400 feet in length. Also by 1914 siding accommodation had been laid, with a large warehouse 500 feet long by 100 feet wide, equipped for the handling of all types of miscellaneous goods.

The hydraulic cranes located on the South Quay were numbered 32, 34, 35 and 36; they were of the movable type, with luffing jibs and a lifting capacity of 3 tons and 3 cwt; similar to these were numbers 44 to 51, also of the movable type with luffing jibs, but capable of lifting 6, 4 and 2 ton weights. The remaining cranes, numbers 33, 37 and 42, were also of the movable type with lifting capacities of 6, 4 and 2 tons and luffing jibs, and finally there was one crane with a lifting capacity of 10, 6½ and 3¼ tons.

In 1934 a petrol-driven mobile crane was purchased by the GWR for use in the sheds on this quay. In the same year five electric capstans and 29 reels were installed to assist with the haulage of the railway wagons and the movable cranes.

Oil tanks wagons destined for Brazil being loaded aboard at South Quay in October 1929. These eight-wheeled wagons are probably of 20 tons tare, and would have had a wheel gauge of 3 ft 3⅜ ins, or 5 ft 3 ins if they were destined for Central Brazil. Made by the Gloucester Wagon Company, they are from a consignment ordered by the Anglo Mexican Petroleum Company, whose emblem, an ancient Inca Indian sign for good fortune, is seen on the tank sides. *Associated British Ports*

Manning Wardle engine *Assam* being loaded aboard at South Quay in September 1925. Fitted with the Ramsbottom safety valves and of an 1880s design, it is being shipped to the Rio Branco in South America to become Rio Grande engine No 105. *Associated British Ports*

Discharging coils of steel wire and steel bars direct into the waiting wagons via the new electric cranes from Messrs Stothert & Pitt of Bath, seen here next to one of the transit sheds at South Quay in March 1927. *Associated British Ports*

SS *Elmsport* berthed at South Quay in May 1928, with No 5 transit shed in the background on the extreme right. As can be seen, general goods, in this case sacks of grain and pipes, are being transferred aboard ship, the latter from GWR 'Macaw' bogie bolster wagons. The wagon on the left is a GWR five-plank open, numbered 81757; the end-swivel tarpaulin rail can be clearly seen. This rail was officially known as the Williams Patent Sheet Rail, and allowed a tarpaulin sheet to be placed above open wagon loads, thus protecting certain types of goods that might be damaged by rain. The GWR 12 tons tare five-plank open wagon was the mainstay of the GWR fleet for many years, and with this tarpaulin rail fitted it was a very useful merchandise wagon from its introduction in 1901 until the mid-1960s. The box van is of LMS design. *Associated British Ports*

SS *City of Christiania*, built in 1921 and of 4,900 GRT, is seen having 1,800 tons of steel sleepers loaded aboard, while berthed at No 2 section of South Quay, near No 6 transit shed, on 11 May 1928. The steel sleepers are probably en route to a country that has a termite problem, possibly Africa. *Associated British Ports*

A cargo of Russian timber being discharged from the Russian vessel *Dvinoles* at berth in South Dock circa 1930. The vessel behind is the SS *Sunmoss*. The Stothert & Pitt cranes are unloading into former GWR five-plank open wagons, some of which are for internal dock use only. Wagon number 067264 in the centre carries the inscription 'For use of sand', and 'Grabs only'. *Associated British Ports*

This vessel berthed at South Quay is discharging raw sugar into railway wagons in September 1933. The wagons seen nearest the camera are again GWR five-plank opens, while those behind are covered with LMS and LNER tarpaulins. The wagon partly seen on the left is a 12-ton Southern Railway vehicle. *Associated British Ports*

The New Zealand liner *Remvera*, built in 1911 and of 11,300 GRT, embarking passengers at South Quay in 1936. She was sunk off Kinnaird Head four years later in August 1940, probably by a German submarine. *Associated British Ports*

The SS *Seapool* at berth near No 6 transit shed at South Quay on 23 August 1950, taking aboard Austin motor cars, fitted with left hand drive. The lifting technique in use by the crane nearest the camera can be seen to differ from the technique used behind. Pipes are being loaded aboard from former GWR 30 tons tare 'Macaw' bogie bolster wagons. Originally these wagons were built for the Taff Vale Railway, and in 1923 passed into GWR ownership. They were ideally suited for the carriage of wood, trees, telegraph poles and rails, as well as pipes. The example seen here is fitted with the updated type of oval buffers, while the original round buffers can be seen on the far wagon. Judging by the insignia on the ship's funnel, this vessel belongs to the Canadian Pacific Steamship Company. *Associated British Ports*

Cattle wagons discharging a shipment of bulls, en route to the Argentine, at South Quay in May 1952. This Hereford bull seems to be a little cautious about descending the ramp. The cage in front will be used to contain him as he is lifted aboard ship. The person on the ramp is holding a rope attached to a ring through the bull's nose, while the rest of the dockers look ready to flee if things don't go to plan! The van nearest the camera is a two-axle, 3-ton-load horse box van, numbered M42400. Also in the rake is another horse box and four passenger train cattle vans. *Associated British Ports*

Cars for export being unloaded from railway vans via the unloading ramp at the end of a siding next to No 8 transit shed at South Quay circa 1952. The van is a GWR 'Python'-type covered carriage van. *Associated British Ports*

The Salvage Factory

About 1915 the railway lines leading to the south side of South Dock were extended to serve the newly built Salvage Factory (also known as the Box Factory). Mainly staffed by women workers, it was used for the reconditioning of shell cases and ammunition boxes, as well as many other items that were returned from the battlefields of France and Belgium during the First World War. Because of the distance from the factory to the dock entrance, the ANDR provided a train service between the two points for the women workers.

By 1934 the GWR had purchased the Salvage Factory, by then known as the Box Factory, and the 486,800 square feet of floor space was to be sub-let for the storage and general handling of imports and exports. Today one-third of this factory area is owned by the firm of Bowaters, the remainder becoming the new No 8 transit shed. This photograph shows the Factory's covered loading platform circa 1929. The dock gates platform can still be seen in Messrs Braithwaites works yard, which is now known as Rocord Limited. *Associated British Ports*

East Quay

This quay was built during 1904 and was situated, as its name suggests, on the east side of the South Dock; it was in use within that year, having a berth of 800 feet. By 1914 it was equipped with eight powerful hydraulic cranes; numbers 20, 22, 23, 24, 25 and 27 were of the movable type with luffing jibs and a lifting capacity of 3 tons 3 cwt, while numbers 21 and 26 were similar but lifted 3 tons and 6 tons when needed.

Also on this quay was a brick-built warehouse 200 feet long and 70 feet wide, the floor of which consisted of a platform for the under-cover loading and unloading of railway wagons; this platform projected from the warehouse, allowing easy handling of traffic between the building and the shipping at East Quay.

Right A sketch of SS *City of Paris* embarking passengers and loading general cargo while berthed at East Quay, South Dock, circa 1913. Note the temporary wooden-planked walkway across the railway lines, complete with handrails. *ANDR booklet of 1916*

Below American troops disembarking at East Quay at the end of the First World War, with a troop train waiting to take them away to the transit camps. In the foreground can be seen onlookers, possibly dockers, with more than one wishing that it was his son that was returning home. On the hull of the troopship can be seen the zigzag camouflage that was designed to break up a ship's outline. *Associated British Ports*

A large vessel at berth at East Quay Circa 1914. Three lines of tracks can be seen alongside the hydraulic cranes next to No 3 transit shed, as these warehouses were called by the GWR. On the right, suspended on a bracket, is a very good example of the early type of electric lights in use. Also in view are some GWR open plank wagons with one in the process of being unsheeted. *Associated British Ports*

Another sketch showing what could almost be a market scene, circa 1913. Actually it is prize-winning pedigree cattle, possibly Herefords, being shipped on to the SS *Spencer* en route to South America for breeding. *ANDR booklet of 1916*

In 1919 special passenger trains were run by the ANDR to East Quay to connect with vessels of the Royal Mail Company, especially the SS *Ebro*, which was a regular visitor to these docks. This photograph shows the passenger train on the left, with the *Ebro* at the quayside, taking on passengers en route for South America. Hydraulic crane number 23 is nearest the camera. *Associated British Ports*

This photograph was taken under wartime censorship controls, and shows an unidentified area of the Alexandra Docks, possibly East Quay, on 21 July 1945, shortly before the end of the Second World War. It shows a shipment of Valentine tanks awaiting dispatch aboard ship; as can be seen these were carried to Newport on LMS low-loading wagons from the Vickers Armstrong factory in Birmingham. Two years earlier these tanks would have been sent to Burma, but at this period in the war, having been surpassed by the British Churchill and the American Sherman tanks, they will possibly be on their way to Greece. They are in drab green, with no squadron markings. *Associated British Ports*

The northern section of East Quay, known as Middle Quay, is the location of Nos 3 and 4 transit sheds. This photograph, taken on 17 June 1905, shows that the construction of Messrs Armstrong Whitworth's new hydraulic cranes is complete and they are ready for work. No 3 transit shed is half-completed.

Today this part of East Quay handles banana traffic from Jamaica and other parts of the West Indies, and citrus fruits from Israel. *Associated British Ports*

The SS *River Afton* discharging iron ore via the travelling cranes at Middle Quay in March 1954. In the background is No 3 transit shed, with engine No 666, originally Alexandra Dock engine No 34, hauling the train. This 0-6-0 tank engine was built by Messrs Kerr Stuart and is seen here a short time before its withdrawal in 1955.
Associated British Ports

West Quay

The ANDR booklet compiled by Mr Macaulay on 30 July 1906, which describes the work done on the South Dock extension, also contains a most descriptive study of the working arrangements as well as the structure of the docks' coaling hoists, and makes very interesting reading:

'The substructures of the coal tips already referred to will consist in each case of a massive tower of solid concrete, about 56 feet long by 35 feet wide, and will have a height of 56 feet, the foundation being carried down to the hard stratum, well below the level of the dock bottom, and the top rising to the quay level. The space intervening between the top of the tower and the edge of the dock slope is to be spanned by steel girders resting on intermediate brick piers and carrying a double line of rails on which the full wagons will be run to the cradle of the hoist.

'Above these girders and partly supported thereon, a viaduct of steel resting on trestles of the same materials will serve to convey the empty wagons to their respective sidings. Where the viaduct crosses the quay its trestles will be carried on substantial bases of brindle, brickwork and concrete, supported in case of any subsidence to the newly formed dock slope by whole timber pitch pine piles of great length driven to the hard sub stratum.

'Each coal hoist will be provided with a turntable and two weighbridges, one for the full, and one for the empty wagons. The full wagons will be run to the weighbridge down a "gravity" siding with carefully proportioned gradients, thence they will be drawn to the hoists by hydraulic power, hoisted, tipped, and returned over the viaduct over the empties siding, gravity being again the motive power. A total length of seven miles of gravity sidings will be provided, for the present, in addition to the line running alongside the dock.'

The types of cargo handled by these docks was quite varied and by 1904 consisted of general cargo, railway material, tin plate and corrugated tin, as well as coal. The latter was not only from the coalfields of the Rhondda, Aberdare and Merthyr areas, but also from the Forest of Dean and the Monmouthshire coalfields. It was brought into the docks by the Monmouthshire Railway & Canal Company as well as the ANDR's own PC&N line from Pontypridd.

The method of coal shipping at these docks was a combination of high and low level working:

'The wagon of coal is run from the sidings to the hoists at quay level, lifted to the necessary tipping height, and discharged, but instead of returning the empty wagon to the same level it is returned along a separate overhead way, carried on pillars to the hoists. Whilst the empty wagon is thus being dealt with, well away from the road for the full ones, the next full one is being brought to the cradle of the hoist, and when this has returned to ground level, the wagon is immediately run on, and the whole process repeated. It will thus be seen that the loading is practically a continuous cycle, limited solely by the use of anti-breakage boxes with the first portion of the cargo and the rate of "trimming" in the holds, and the handling of full and empty wagons, to and from the hoists.'

Before the decline of the coal exports from South Wales these docks contained a tremendous amount of siding accommodation, covering a total of 50 miles, with three low-level lines leading to each hoist. Vessels were loaded by day and night, and in 1901 Mr Macaulay directed that the old charge of 1d per ton for the shipment of coal by night was to cease; although this meant the loss of extra revenue, it was a shrewd move as the extra shipments that followed tripled the revenue.

In 1914 the charges for the use of coal hoists were set at 2d per ton, and the weighing of coal or coke was 1 farthing per ton; for the shipment of stones by crane at the coal hoists a minimum charge of 2s 6d per hour was made.

For the lifting of cargoes weighing a total of 30 tons, the charges per lift were as follows: lifts not exceeding 3 tons, 3d per ton; 3 tons but not exceeding 5 tons, 1s 6d; rising to 6s 6d for a lift of 25 tons but not exceeding 30 tons.

Above The coal hoists at West Quay circa 1923 - that nearest the camera is number 18, followed by 17, 16, 15 and 14 in the distance.

The vessel at number 18 hoist is the *City of Messina*, and judging by the amount of coal heaped above the hold the crew are hard at work shovelling to distribute this load evenly. On the left can be seen one of the open plank colliery wagons of the Tredegar Iron & Coal Company, from the Mclaren pits at New Tredegar. The motor car appears to be of 1920 vintage. *Associated British Ports*

Left The special digging-out appliance fitted for use inside coal wagons to free coal that had not dropped free of the wagon. Circa 1927. *Associated British Ports*

Above The new transverser type of coal hoist under construction circa 1930. *Associated British Ports*

Right GWR 20-ton coal wagons at the number 20 coaling hoist, which was separate from the others, circa 1930. It was near this hoist that a proposed dry dock was to be constructed, situated at the bottom end of South Dock. Today this area is the reception point for Japanese cars being imported into Wales, with three massive car terminals. This part of the docks is an ideal position to receive the NYK and Wallenius vessels that deliver cars to Newport Docks as they can make use of the constant water levels. *Associated British Ports*

ALEXANDRA *As issued 5th October 1908*
(NEWPORT AND SOUTH WALES) DOCKS AND RAILWAY.

Regulations as to Private Owners' Waggons.

The Alexandra (Newport and South Wales) Docks and Railway Company hereby give notice that the working of Private Owners' Waggons on the Company's Railways is subject to the following Regulations : --

1.—The owners of all new, reconstructed or converted vehicles intended to work upon the Alexandra (Newport and South Wales) Docks and Railway, must, before they are brought into use, communicate with Mr. T. W. R. Pearson, Locomotive and Waggon Superintendent, Alexandra Docks, Newport, Mon., so that he may have them inspected without unreasonable delay, and, if built, reconstructed or converted (as the case may be) in accordance with the Railway Clearing House Standard Specification, register plates, as described in the Specification, shall be forthwith affixed to each.

2.—The name and Address of the Owner or Lessee, the Waggon-number, and the tare, shall be painted conspicuously on both sides of the waggon ; the maximum load must also be clearly indicated on both sides of the waggon.

When waggons are let on hire the Lessee will, for the purpose of these Regulations, be regarded as the Owner.

Provided that when the hire is for a term of not less than three months, the name and address of the Lessee shall be painted or exhibited on a board or plate on both sides of the waggon, and that when the hire is for less than three months, the name and address of the Lessee shall either be so painted, or exhibited on a card (other than the waggon-label), on both sides of the waggon.

3.—The Owners or Lessees, as the case may be, shall keep their waggons in good working condition, and have them properly lubricated and examined and put into good repair before being tendered to the Company for transit.

4.—The Company may remove the register plates from any waggon if wheels, axles or any other materials of less dimensions or strength than those provided for by the Railway Clearing House Standard Specification are afterwards substituted in contravention of the conditions of the said Specification.

5.—If in transit any defect should be observed, which for the proper and safe working it is necessary to repair before the vehicles are allowed to proceed further, the Company may, with the consent of the Owners, make such repairs, and charge them with all expenses incurred in effecting the same.

6.—In pursuance of the rules made by the Board of Trade under the provisions of the Railway Employment (Prevention of Accidents) Act, 1900, when it is necessary in the ordinary course of business that any label or direction as to destination or consignee shall be placed upon any railway waggon, such label or direction must be placed on both sides of such waggon ; and no Private Owner's Waggon will be accepted for conveyance on the Company's railway unless so labelled or directed on both sides.

All waggon Owners, representatives of waggon Companies and their repairers, when labelling defective waggons at railway stations and depôts shall clearly set forth on the labels the station or siding from and to which the waggons are required to travel, and hand in a proper Consignment Note or written forwarding instructions.

7.—When waggons, for the purpose of repair, are required to be shunted into and out of Railway companies sidings and/or into and out of premises in the occupation of [Private Waggon Repairers a charge of 6d. per waggon will be made for such services, except where a higher charge is now made, in which case such higher charge shall be the maximum charge under these regulations.

Siding rent will be chargeable to the Owner, or his agent, in respect of standing room for any waggon detained at a station or siding for repairs at the rate of 6d. per waggon per day, which will be calculated from the expiration of three days, exclusive of the date of the advice note, Sundays and Bank Holidays, from the time the waggon is placed at the disposal of the Owner or Repairer, and to terminate when the waggon is labelled for despatch after repair.

8.—Any authorised servant of the Company may detain any waggon which may appear to him unfit to run until it has been put into proper repair and passed by one of the Company's waggon examiners or inspectors.

9.—The Company will not be responsible for any damage to Private Owners' Waggons left unprotected in an imperfect state by the Owners, nor for any injury that may occur to waggon repairers, who will be required to execute an indemnity before they are allowed to work on the Company's premises.

10.—Private Owners' Waggons running over the Railway Company's lines must not, apart from a reasonable description of the contents of the waggon, be used for advertising purposes, but the Railway Company will not object to a description (to be approved by them) of a product of the Owner's manufacture being painted thereon.

11.—*Nothing contained in these Regulations shall prejudice or affect any legal liability to each other of the actual Owners or Lessees of Waggons and the Railway Companies.*

JOHN MACAULAY,

General Manager.

Newport, Mon.,
October, 1908.

Left 'Regulations as to Private Owners' Waggons', October 1908.
Associated British Ports

Above Coal for shipment abroad circa 1930, shown here at the Tredegar Park Sidings, one of the Alexandra Docks numerous yards. The wagons bearing the initials 'EV' are from the Ebbw Vale collieries, while those marked 'JL' are from the John Lancaster Company, which had collieries at Blaina, Cwmtillery and Griffin. *Associated British Ports*

Above This scene from about 1923 gives one a good idea of the vastness of West Quay, with its extensive coal lines leading to the towering coal hoists. The photographer is facing north-east towards the Junction Cut direction; nearest the camera is hoist number 19, with numbers 18, 17, 16, 15 and 14 in that order beyond. To the left of hoist number 19, in the far distance, can be seen the coaling hoists of North Dock.

The West Quay hoists eventually fell into disuse when the decision was made to transfer the coal trade of South Wales from Newport Docks to Barry and Swansea Docks instead, and the removal of the hoists and roads started in August 1964. While sad, it has to be admitted that to keep abreast of modern developments changes have to be made, and for the sake of the docks Newport had to change. Today this area is covered by massive timber stocks, some stacked almost 20 feet high, supervised and controlled by the experienced staff of timber merchants MBM Ltd (Macmillan, Bloodel & Meyer), whose Forest Products Terminal is one of the largest of its type in Europe, handling products mainly from the forests of Canada. *Associated British Ports*

COPY

ALEXANDRA (N. & S.W.) DOCKS AND RAILWAY.

——

NOTICE OF INCREASE OF DOCK RATES, DUES AND CHARGES

NOTICE IS HEREBY GIVEN that pursuant to power conferred on the Company by an Order of the Board of Trade dated the third day of June, 1918, the Alexandra (Newport & South Wales) Docks and Railway Company intend to increase the charges for tipping and weighing coal and coke by machinery to the sum of sixpence per ton and to increase all other Dock Statutory Rates Dues and Charges by Fifty per cent. Such increased rates dues and charges are to come into operation as from midnight of August 31st, 1918, and particulars of the same can be obtained at the Office of the Company, Newport, Mon.

BY ORDER.

J. H. VICKERY,

General Manager.

Alexandra (Newport & South Wales) Docks & Railway
Company.

Newport, Mon.
August 21st, 1918.

Left Increase of dock rates, dues and charges, 21 August 1918. *Associated British Ports*

An aerial view giving a clear indication of the position of Alexandra Docks. The River Usk winds its way past the town of Newport, which is situated to the left of the Transporter Bridge (top left of the picture at the base of the first bend of the river); on the right-hand side at the mouth of the Usk are the private Mountstuart Dry Docks. In the centre left of the photograph is North Dock, while the River Ebbw is seen in the bottom left-hand corner.

South Dock is in the centre of the photograph, with the piers of South Lock reaching out like feelers into the Bristol Channel; the west pier is on the left. Between the outer and inner gates of the lock can be seen the brick-built South Lock Power Station, which accommodated an economiser, water softening and feed pump house in one building, and in the other pumping, electric lighting and power house. The most prominent feature is the chimney stack, 187 feet high.

This 1935 photograph was duplicated and issued along with others to the German Luftwaffe bombing crews during 1940-42, the only difference being that compass points were superimposed. The photographs were collected after their briefings by the crews together with detailed written instructions in the correct folder for the area they were bombing; the Newport Docks folder was numbered GB7, BB27, number 2. The idea was that if the aircraft overshot their target they would fly onwards to the next one and use their bombs on that; for example, the next targets might be GB7, BB27 number 13, Messrs J. Lysaght Limited, steelworks; GB7, BB27 number 16, British Aluminium Company Works; and if not them, then GB7, BB27, number 61, the Neptune Machine Works.

The crews were also issued with a booklet of key installations that they could blow up, acting as saboteurs, if they were shot down. Many Germans posing as tourists took scenic photographs around England and Wales before the Second World War, and key installations would be included in the background. These 'holiday snaps' were then enlarged, ready for issue when war broke out.
Associated British Ports

Disaster and heroism

Disaster struck on 2 July 1909 when a team of 53 men and boys employed as navvies and timbermen were working in the outer wall trench of the south-west wing of part of the new South Dock. At approximately 5.20 pm, a matter of minutes before the end of their shift, a tremendous cracking sound was heard coming from the huge support timbers, and within a few seconds they were catapulted into the air before falling into the trench and on to the men 50 feet below. Only one man was visible amongst the debris of fallen timbers, earth, wagons and steam cranes - it was as if the earth had just opened up, one eyewitness stated.

Immediately the cave-in was heard, railway engines all over the extension workings began to sound their whistles to summon help, and within minutes rescuers had arrived and the operation to save those trapped was under way. However, the collapse was of a colossal scale, and time was against the rescuers.

The first immediate danger was from the collapsed steam cranes, which still had their boilers lit. Unless those fires were extinguished the men entombed beneath the twisted and mangled timbers would be burned to death.

A hero of the disaster was Thomas Lewis, a young lad of 14; he was a newspaper boy whose father worked on the docks as a stevedore. The noise of the steam whistles seemed to carry for miles, and Wallis Street, where Thomas lived, was like many other streets near the docks soon filled with talk of the disaster.

An injured man was found alive amongst the wreckage of broken beams and twisted metal, but the hole to reach him was narrow, too narrow for the broad-shouldered men of the rescue teams. Young Thomas went down, twisting his body as he worked his way through the fissure, crawling inch by inch until he finally reached the trapped man. With an effort in that maze of timber he started to free him, but before he was able to lead him to

The collapsed trench, seen here on 4 July 1909, two days after the disaster, looking northwards. In view are some of the ANDR managers and members of the Board of Inspectors. The gentleman to the left of the group of four is Mr Macaulay, ANDR General Manager - he appears to be wiping his face. At the far end of the trench is what appears to be a cameraman and possibly members of the press. In the middle distance can be seen one of the contractors' engines with a short-wheelbase carriage attached, probably for the use of the Inspectorate. *Newport Resource Centre*

Above Another view of the disaster area, on 5 July 1909. The tidal water has flooded the collapsed workings. *Associated British Ports*

Below By 6 July the work to fill in the collapse is still in operation. The contractors' side-tip wagons and rotary cement mixer can be clearly seen. A large amount of water is still visible. *Associated British Ports*

safety another fall started. With timbers starting to move it was all Thomas could do to scramble back upwards to safety before the narrow gap collapsed.

As darkness fell that night, hundreds of townsfolk watched as 500 men worked under the light of scores of acetylene flares, struggling, wrestling and heaving at the fallen 14-inch-thick timber mainstays and the 12-inch-thick cross-pieces, broken and twisted by the force that had caused their collapse.

Rescue operations continued throughout the night into Saturday 3 July, but by noon there was very little hope of anyone buried still being alive, and by the afternoon the tidal water began to seep over the excavated ground and eventually enter the collapsed trench. The teams had managed to recover five bodies and rescue 15 men, alive but injured; one of these later died from his injuries.

The next day, Sunday 4 July, the collapsed trench was full of water, and with the approval of the coroner work

began immediately to fill it in. On 8 July a funeral service was held on the site of the disaster, attended by over 2,000 mourners, friends and families that had waited in vain. By 10 July the filling in of the trench was completed.

A year later, in December 1910, while work was under way to sink blocks of stone near the area of the disaster, a further 17 bodies were removed, leaving 16 still buried beneath the South Dock.

As a mark of his heroism Thomas Lewis was invited to tea at Buckingham Palace, and while there he was awarded the Albert Medal, Britain's highest award for civilian bravery in peace-time. The inscription reads 'For Gallantry in saving life on land'.

In the cemetery of St Woolos Church, Newport, is a monument to the dead, erected by Messrs Easton Gibb & Son, carrying a plaque that reads quite simply: 'As a tribute of respect to the memory of those 39 workmen who lost their lives in the trench disaster at the new dock works on the 2nd July 1909.'

Thomas Lewis, the boy hero of this terrible disaster. When hope was still fresh in the hearts of those whose men and sons were trapped, this lad risked his life to try and save them, being at the time only 14 years of age. Photographed here at the disaster area on 4 July 1909, he died in April 1969. *Newport Resource Centre*

Types of cranes used in the docks from 1898 to the present day

Builder	Date built	Number and type	Scrapped
Armstrong Whitworth Co	1898	One: fixed, hydraulic, fixed jib, 30 ton lift	1963
Armstrong Whitworth Co	Unknown	Three: mobile, hydraulic, fixed jib, 2 ton lift	July 1959
Armstrong Whitworth Co	1905	Three: movable, hydraulic, fixed jib, one of 3 to 1½ ton lift, two of 6 to 3 ton lift	1957
East Ferry Road Engineering Co	1909	Nine: movable, hydraulic, luffing, 3 to 1½ ton lift	1957 (2), May 1960 (1), Sept 1959 (6)
East Ferry Road Engineering Co	1909	Three: movable, hydraulic, luffing, 6 and 4 to 2 ton lift	Sept 1959 (2), third transferred to Port Talbot Docks
Hydraulic Engineering Co	1914	Six: movable, hydraulic, luffing, 3 ton to 27 cwt lift	May 1960
Armstrong Whitworth Co	1918	Two: movable, hydraulic, luffing, one of 10 and 6½ to 3¼ ton lift, one of 6 and 4 to 2 ton lift	1957 (1), 1959 (1)
Stothert & Pitt Ltd	1925-31	22: portal, electric, luffing, 3 ton lift	Early to mid-1960s
GWR	1942-44	Four: portal, electric, luffing, 3 ton lift	1973-76
Stothert & Pitt Ltd	1927 (2), 1942 (1)	Three: portal, electric, level, luffing, 6 ton lift	1972
Clyde Engineering Co	1925-28	Three: portal electric, luffing 6 ton lift	1972
Stothert & Pitt Ltd	1950	One: portal, diesel-electric, luffing, 6 ton lift	
Stothert & Pitt Ltd	1959-60	Six: portal, electric, level, luffing, 3 ton lift	Early 1980s
Stothert & Pitt Ltd	1951	Four: portal, electric, level, luffing and grabbing, 11½ and 10 ton lift	1970s (2), remaining two refurbished in 1987 and still in use
Stothert & Pitt Ltd	1962-64	Five: portal, level, luffing and grabbing, 11½ and 10 ton lift	Mid-1980s (1), two refurbished in 1994, four still in use
Stothert & Pitt Ltd	1965	Two: portal, electric, level, luffing, 25 ton lift	Still in use
John Henderson & Co, Aberdeen	1969	One: electric derrick, 32 ton lift	1993
Paececo Vickers	1969	One: Portainer, 30 ton lift	Transferred to Hull Docks late 1970s
J. H. Wilson	1918	Four: steam travelling cranes, 10 ton lift	1961 (3), 1968 (1)
Grafton Engineering Co	1890	One: steam travelling crane, 5 ton lift	1968
Thomas Smith Rodley	1953	One: steam travelling crane, 10 ton lift	1980s
Thomas Smith Rodley	1963	One: diesel rail crane, 5 ton lift	1980s; donated to railway society
Mannesmann Demag Ltd	1995	One: mobile harbour crane, 45 tonne lift	Still in use

Current (1995) cranage facilities at Alexandra Docks:

13: 6 and 3 ton lift

Six: 11½ ton lift (general cargo) to 10 ton lift (grabbing)

One: 10 ton lift (general cargo) to 8 ton lift (grabbing)

Two: 25 ton lift (John Boyd)

NEW—NEW HAND-BOOK OF RAILWAY STATIONS, &c. 506

Station Accommodation	Crane Power (Tons Cwts)	Stations, &c.	County	Company	Position
G P	L H	1 10	Newpark— Murieston Siding	Edinburgh	L.M.S. (Cal.)	Holytown and Edinburgh.
			New Park Pit	Edinburgh	L.M.S. (Cal.)	Newpark.
			New Penshaw Siding	Yorks	L.N.E. (N.E.)	Same as Low Moor Ironworks Co. (Leeds).
			New Penshaw Siding	Durham	L.N.E. (N.E.)	Penshaw.
			New Peterboro' Brick Sidings	Hunts	L.N.E. (G.N.)	Fencehouses. See London Brick Co., and Forders, Ltd. (Fletton).
G P		1 10	New Pool Colliery	Carmarth	G.W. (B.P.G.V.)	Burry Port.
			Newport	Essex	L.N.E. (G.E.)	Cambridge and Bishops Stortford.
			Barnard Bros.' Siding	Essex	L.N.E. (G.E.)	Newport.
			Wenn's, T. H., Siding	Essex	L.N.E. (G.E.)	Newport.
G P F L			Newport	I. of W.	Southern (I.W.C.)	Cowes and Ryde.
G P F L	L H C	3 0		I. of W.	Southern (F.Y.N.)	Newport Junction and Carisbrooke.
G P F L	L H C	8 0		I. of W.	Southern (I.S.W.)	Carisbrooke and Watchingwell.
G P F L	L H C	2 0	Gunville Siding	Mayo	G.S. (M.G.W.)	Westport and Achill.
			Newport— Adams, A. R., & Son's Pill Bank Iron Works	Mon	G.W.	Over Tredegar Estate Lines.
			Adams, W., & Co.	Mon	G.W.	Pilgwenlly Coal Yard.
G P		30 0	Alexandra Docks (GW ADR)	Mon	G.W. (A.D.R.-G.W.)	Newport.
			Anglo-American Oil Co.'s Siding	Mon	G.W.	Branch from Dock Street.
			Arrol's (Sir Wm.), Ltd.	Mon	G.W. / G.W. (A.D.R.-G.W.)	Liverpool Wharf. Rhoswen Wharf. Alexandra Docks.
			Arrow Fuel Co.'s Works	Mon	G.W.	Over Tredegar Estate Lines.
			Bailey's, C. H., Engineering Works	Mon	G.W.	Alexandra Docks.
			Bailey, C. H. Graham & Co.'s Dry Dock	Mon	G.W.	Carngethin Wharf.
			Baker Siding	Mon	G.W.	Nettlefold's Branch.
			Basic Slag & Phosphate Co., Ltd. Siding	Mon	G.W.	Dock Street and Mill Street.
			Batcheler & Co.'s Timber Yd.	Mon	G.W. (A.D.R.-G.W.)	East Mendalgief Sidings (Alexandra Dock). Town Dock.
			Batchelor, T. B. & S. & Co. (Timber Importers)	Mon	G.W.	Dock Street.
			Blaina Wharf	Mon	G.W.	Dock Street.
			Bolt Street Timber Yd. Sida.	Mon	G.W.	Over Tredegar Estate Lines.
			Braithwaite & Co.'s Neptune Works	Mon	G.W.	Branch from East Usk Junction.
			British Mannesman Tube Co., Ltd. Sidings	Mon	G.W.	Branch from Dock Street.
			British Petroleum Co., Ltd. Sid. (Quiet Woman's Row)	Mon	G.W.	Branch from Dock Street.
			Burt, Boulton & Heywood's Timber Creosote Yard.	Mon	G.W. (A.D.R.-G.W.)	Alexandra Docks.
			Bute Works Supply Co.'s Sid.	Mon	G.W. (A.D.R.-G.W.)	Alexandra Docks.
			Cambrian Wagon Co., Ltd.	Mon	G.W.	Dock Parade. Over Tredegar Estate Lines.
			Carngethin Wharf	Mon	G.W.	Town Dock.
			Cashmore, John— Siding	Mon	G.W.	Blains Wharf.
			Siding	Mon	G.W.	Rhymney Wharf.
			Siding	Mon	G.W.	Russell's Wharf.
			Central Works	Mon	G.W.	Dock Street and Mill Street.
			Cheshire, T., & Co.'s Warehouse	Mon	G.W. (A.D.R.-G.W.)	Alexandra Docks.
			Chaderill Wharf	Mon	G.W.	Dock Street and Mill Street.
			Clapp's Wharf	Mon	G.W.	Town Dock.
			Clarence Wharf Saw Mills.	Mon	G.W.	East Usk Wharf.
			Clark, Geo., & Co.	Mon	G.W.	Earl Usk Wharf.
			Clements, Jas., & Co.	Mon	G.W.	Gloucester Wharf.
			Collier, Chas., Ltd.	Mon	G.W.	Herbert's Siding.
			Co-operative Wholesale Society Mills	Mon	G.W.	Town Dock.
			Cork Wharf	Mon	G.W.	Branch near Dock Street.
			Corpn. Electric Power Sta.	Mon	G.W.	East Usk Wharf.
			Courtybella Coal Yard	Mon	G.W.	Over Tredegar Estate Lines.
			Coverack Coal Yard (J. J. P. Isitt)	Mon	G.W.	East Usk Wharf.

HAND-BOOK OF RAILWAY STATIONS, &c. NEW—NEW 507

Station Accommodation	Crane Power (Tons Cwts)	Stations, &c.	County	Company	Position
			NEWPORT—continued. Davies, H., & Son	Mon	G.W.	East Usk Wharf.
			Dibble, J. O., & Co.	Mon	G.W.	Rock Wharf. Over Tredegar Estate, Lines.
			Dock Foundry (C. & A. Fontaine).	Mon	G.W.	Over Tredegar Estate Lines.
			Dock Parade Sidings	Mon	G.W.	Over Tredegar Estate Lines.
G	F L	5 0	Dock Street (G.W.)	Mon	G.W.-B.& M. / L.M.S. (L.N.W.)	Cwmbran and Waterloo Junction. Over G.W. from Hereford.
			Dos Nail Works (Corden&Co.)	Mon	G.W.	Dock Street and Cwmbran.
			East Usk Branch	Mon	G.W.	High Street and Llanwern.
			East Usk Wharf (Great Western Wharf)	Mon	G.W.	High Street and Lliswerry.
			Ebbw Vale Steel, Iron, and Coal Co.— Ebbw Vale Iron Wharf	Mon	G.W.	Dock Street and Mill Street.
			Mariner's Wharf (Sleeper Plant Works)	Mon	G.W.	Dock Street and Mill Street.
			Pontypool Wharf	Mon	G.W.	Dock Street and Mill Street.
			Victoria Wharf (C. D. Phillips)	Mon	G.W.	Dock Street and Mill Street.
			Emlyn Foundry	Mon	G.W.	Dock Street and Mill Street.
			Evans, William, Orindan Glass Works (G.W.)	Mon	G.W.-L.M.S. (L.N.W.)	Dock Street and Cwmbran. Ship Siding. Over Tredegar Estate Lines.
			Finlay Conveyor	Mon	G.W.	East Usk Wharf.
			Brithdir Yard	Mon	G.W.	Over Tredegar Estate Lines.
			Fleming Composition Co.	Mon	G.W.	Loco. Yard, Dock Street.
			Fontaine's Foundry	Mon	G.W.	Gloucester Wharf.
			Pond & Pickford's Timber Yd.	Mon	G.W.	Dock Street and Cwmbran.
			Fruit Distributing Co., Ltd.	Mon	G.W.	Moderator Wharf.
			Gas Works	Mon	G.W.	Dock Street and Cwmbran.
			Gilchrist, R., & Co.'s Siding	Mon	G.W. (A.D.R.-G.W.)	Lisearth Wharf.
			Goss, A. J. T., & Co.	Mon	G.W.	Dock Parade. Over Tredegar Estate Lines.
			Gould's Foundries, Ltd.	Mon	G.W.	Same as East Usk Wharf.
			Great Western Wharf	Mon	G.W.	Same as East Usk Wharf (Great Western Wharf) Lines.
			Greenland, G., & Son.	Mon	G.W.	Herbert's Siding.
			Guest, Keen & Nettlefold— Imperial Iron & Steel Wks	Mon	G.W.	On East Usk Wharf (Great Western Wharf) Lines.
			Patent Nut & Bolt Works	Mon	G.W.	Dock Street and Mill Street.
			Hall Lewis, & Co.'s Wagon Works	Mon	G.W.	Penner Wharf.
			Happerfield & Willans	Mon	G.W.	East Usk Wharf.
			Harding, G. F.	Mon	G.W.	Pill Wharf.
			Heeley & Peart, Ltd.	Mon	G.W.	Branch from East Usk Junction.
			Herbert's Siding	Mon	G.W.	High Street and Caerleon.
G	P F L	8 0	High Street (G.W.)	Mon	G.W. (B.& M.) / L.M.S. (L.N.W.)	Gloucester and Cardiff. Over G.W. from Nine Mile Point Jn.
			Hodge, Ralph, & Co.	Mon	G.W.	Herbert's Siding.
			Hodson's Concrete Products, Ltd.	Mon	G.W.	Lysaght & Co.'s Siding.
			Houlder Bros. & Co.'s Warehouse	Mon	G.W.	
			International Brattice Cloth Co.	Mon	G.W. (A.D.R.-G.W.)	Alexandra Dock. King's Parade.
			Isca Foundry Co.	Mon	G.W.	Estate Lines. Over Tredegar
			James & Emanuel	Mon	G.W.	Branch from East Usk Junction.
			Jordan's Foundry (Pill grenilly Foundry).	Mon	G.W. (A.D.R.-G.W.)	Branch from Dock Street.
			King's Parade Sidings	Mon	G.W.	High Street and Mill Street.
			Lewis, C., & Co.	Mon	G.W.	Town Dock.
			Llwnarth Street Electric Light Works	Mon	G.W.	Over Tredegar Estate Lines.
			Lianarth Wharf	Mon	G.W.	Liverpool Wharf.
			Lynch, J.	Mon	G.W. (A.D.R.-G.W.)	Dock Street and Mill Street.
			Lysaght's Orb Iron Works	Mon	G.W.	Town Dock.
			Mahoney, J., & Co.	Mon	G.W.	Waterloo Wharf. Branch from East Usk Junction. King's Parade. Over Tredegar Estate Lines.

EXPLANATION—G Goods Station. P Passenger and Parcel Station. P* Passenger, but not Parcel or Miscellaneous Traffic. L Live Stock.
F Furniture Vans, Carriages, Portable Engines, and Machines on Wheels. C Carriage by Passenger Train.
H Horse Boxes and Prize Cattle Vans.

508	NEW—NEW	HAND-BOOK OF RAILWAY STATIONS, &c.

STATION ACCOMMODATION	CRANE POWER (Tons Cwts)	STATIONS, &c.	COUNTY	COMPANY	POSITION
		Newport—continued.			
		Mahoney, J., & Co.—	Mon	G.W.	Town Dock.
		Maybury & Co.'s Kubla Works	Mon	G.W.	Clapp's Wharf.
		Maybury's Adamant and Plaster Co.	Mon	G.W.	Pill Wharf.
		Mendalgief Sids (GW ADR)	Mon	G.W.(A.D.R.–G.W.)	Alexandra Docks.
		Mexico Oil & Grease Co.	Mon	G.W.(A.D.R.–B.&M.)	East Usk Wharf.
G	10 0	Mill Street Mileage & Coal Sidings (G.W.)	Mon	G.W. / L.M.S.(L.N.W.)	Dock Street and Cwmbran. / Over G.W. from Hereford.
		Moderator Sidings	Mon	G.W.	Dock Street and Mill Street.
		Moderator Wharf	Mon	G.W.	Dock Street and Mill Street.
		Morris, H., & Co.'s Baltic Oil Works	Mon	G.W.	Town Dock.
		Morris, Wm., Ltd., Dock Parade Wagon Works	Mon	G.W.	Branch from Dock Street.
		Mount Stuart Dry Dock & Shearman's, Ltd.—	Mon	G.W.	Ship Siding. Over Tredegar Estate Lines.
		Dry Dock, West Side	Mon	G.W.(A.D.R.)	Alexandra Dock, West Side.
		North Dock	Mon	G.W.(A.D.R.–G.W.)	Branch from East Usk Junction.
		Eastern Dry Dock	Mon	G.W.(A.D.R.–G.W.)	Dock Street and Mill Street.
		Siding	Mon	G.W.	Dock Street.
		Western Dry Dock	Mon	G.W.	Carngethin Wharf.
		Newport Enamel Slate Co. (Baker, W. A., & Co.)	Mon	G.W.	Rock Wharf. Over Tredegar Estate Lines.
		Newport Foundry Co.	Mon	G.W.	
		Newport (Mon) Cold Storage and Ice Co., Ltd.	Mon	G.W.(A.D.R.–G.W.)	Alexandra Dock.
		Factory and Cold Stores	Mon	G.W.(A.D.R.–G.W.)	Town Dock.
		Fish Wharf	Mon	G.W.	Alexandra Dock.
		Nicholas & Co.'s Timber Yard	Mon		
		Nicholas & Co.'s Timber Yard (Baltic Wharf)	Mon	G.W.	Dock Street and Mill Street.
		Parr, G. W., & Sons	Mon	G.W.	Waterloo Wharf.
		Partridge, Jones & John Paton's Pill Wharf (Newport Adamant & Plaster Co.)	Mon	G.W.	
		Penner Wharf	Mon	G.W.	Branch near Dock Street.
		Phillips & Son's Malt House	Mon	G.W.	Town Dock.
		Phillips, C. D.	Mon	G.W.	Penner Wharf.
		Pillgwenlly Coal Yard	Mon	G.W.	Central Iron Works.
		Pillgwenlly Foundry	Mon	G.W.	Branch near Dock Street.
		Pillgwenlly Wharf	Mon	G.W.	Branch from Dock Street.
		Powell's Town Wharf (Budd & Co.)	Mon	G.W.	Over Tredegar Estate Lines.
		Protheroe's Wharf (G. F. Harding)	Mon	G.W.	Dock Street and Mill Street.
		Rees, F. E.	Mon	G.W.	Branch near Dock Street.
		Rhoewen Wharf	Mon	G.W.	Herbert's Siding.
		Rhymney Wharf	Mon	G.W.	Ship Siding. Over Tredegar Estate Lines.
		Ripley, W., & Co.'s Wagon Wks	Mon	G.W.	Town Dock.
		Risca Wharf	Mon	G.W.	Vipond's Wharf.
		River Coal Shipping Jetties	Mon	G.W.(A.D.R.–G.W.)	Alexandra Docks.
		Rock Wharf	Mon	G.W.	Dock Street.
		Russell's Wharf	Mon	G.W.(A.D.R.–G.W.)	Over Tredegar Estate Lines.
		Sessions & Sons	Mon	G.W.	Town Dock.
		Shell-Mex, Ltd., Oil Depôt.	Mon	G.W.	East Usk Wharf.
		Ship Siding	Mon	G.W.	Town Dock.
		Smith's (Newport) Ltd Star Flour Mills	Mon	G.W.	Branch near Dock Street.
		South Wales Malleable Iron Foundry (Heeley&Peart)	Mon	G.W.	Cuxferhill Wharf.
		Spittle, Thos., Ltd. (Cambrian Foundry)	Mon	G.W.	Branch from East Usk Junction.
		Thomas, A.	Mon	G.W.(A.D.R.–G.W.)	Town Dock.
		Tilley Wharf	Mon	G.W.	Waterloo Wharf. / Town Dock.

EXPLANATIONS—G Goods Station. P Passenger and Parcel Station. P* Passenger, but not Parcel or Miscellaneous Traffic.
F Furniture Vans, Carriages, Portable Engines, and Machines on Wheels. L Live Stock.
H Horse Boxes and Prize Cattle Vans. C Carriages by Passenger Train.

NEW—NEW	HAND-BOOK OF RAILWAY STATIONS, &c.	509

STATION ACCOMMODATION	CRANE POWER (Tons Cwts)	STATIONS, &c.	COUNTY	COMPANY	POSITION
		Newport—continued.			
		Town Dock	Mon	G.W.(A.D.R.–G.W.)	Branch from Dock Street.
		Tredegar Dry Dock & Wharf Co.—			
		Siding	Mon	G.W.	Over Tredegar Estate Lines.
		Siding	Mon	G.W.	Branch from East Usk Station.
		Tredegar Estate Lines	Mon	G.W.	Branch near Dock Street.
G P	5 0	Trott, E. & Son	Mon	G.W.	Tillery Wharf.
G P	2 0	Uskside Engineering Co., Ltd. Siding	Mon	G.W.	Branch near Dock Street.
		Vipond, J. & Co.	Mon	G.W.	Vipond's Wharf.
		Vipond's Wharf	Mon	G.W.	Dock Street and Mill Street.
		Wagon Repairs, Ltd.—	Mon	G.W.(G.W.–A.D.R.)	King's Parade. Over Tredegar Estate [Lines.
		Siding	Mon	G.W.	Town Dock.
		Walker Bros.	Mon	G.W.	Risca Wharf.
		Waterloo Wharf	Mon	G.W.	Ship Siding. Over Tredegar Estate [Lines.
P		Western Navigation Co.Ltd	Mon	G.W.	East Usk Branch.
G		Whitehead Iron and Steel Co.,Ltd.Sid (Courtybella)	Mon	G.W.	Dock Street and Maesglas Junction.
		Williams & Thomas	Mon	G.W.	East Usk Wharf.
G P F L H C		Newport	Salop	L.M.S.(L.N.W.)	Shrewsbury and Stafford.
G P F L H C	5 0	Newport	Yorks	L.N.E.(N.E.)	Stockton and Middlesbrough.
P		Newport (East)	Fife	L.N.E.(N.B.)	Dundee and Tayport.
		Newport (West)	Fife	L.N.E.(N.B.)	Newport (East) and Tayport.
		Newport Gas Works	Fife	L.N.E.(N.B.)	Dundee and Tayport.
		Newport Adamant & Plaster Co.	Mon	G.W.	Same as Partridge, Jones and John Paton, Ltd. Pill Wharf (Newport).
		Newport Enamel Slate Co. (Baker, W. A., & Co.)	Mon	G.W.	Newport.
		Newport Foundry Co.	Yorks	L.N.E.(N.E.)	Middlesbrough.
		Newport Iron Works, Coke Ovens, and Wharf	Mon	G.W.	Newport.
		Newport (Mon) Cold Storage and Ice Co., Ltd.	Yorks	L.N.E.(N.E.)	Middlesbrough.
G P F L H C	5 0	Newport Pagnell	Mon	G.W.(A.D.R.–G.W.)	Newport, Alexandra Dock.
		Fish Wharf	Mon	G.W.	Newport, Town Dock.
		Newport Pagnell	Bucks	L.M.S.(L.N.W.)	Branch from Wolverton.
		Coates & Son's Shipley Wharf	Bucks	L.M.S.(L.N.W.)	Newport Pagnell and Great Linford.
G P F L H C	6 0	Price's Siding	Bucks	L.M.S.(L.N.W.)	Newport Pagnell.
		Newport Rivet Co., Ltd.	Mon	G.W.	Lliswerry.
		Newport Road Sidings	Glamorg'n	G.W.(T.V.)	See Cardiff.
		Newport Wire Works	Yorks	L.N.E.(N.E.)	Middlesbrough.
		Newport Process Co., Ltd.	Middlesex	G.W.	Southall.
G P F L H C	6 0	Newquay	Cornwall	G.W.	Branch from Par.
		British Petroleum Co., Ltd	Cornwall	G.W.	Quintrell Downs Siding.
		Newquay Harbour	Cornwall	G.W.	Extension from Newquay.
		Pollard's Siding	Cornwall	G.W.	Extension from Newquay.
G		Quintrell Downs Siding	Cornwall	G.W.	Newquay and St. Columb Road.
		Stephens & Co.	Cornwall	G.W.	Quintrell Downs Siding.
		Trevemper Siding	Cornwall	G.W.	Devonport.
G P F L H C	1 0	New Quays	Devon	Southern (L.S.W.)	Tolcarn Junc. and Shepherd's Siding.
G P F L H C		New Radnor	Radnor	G.W.	Branch from Titley.
		New Rock Colliery Siding	Somerset	S.&D. Jt.	Chilcompton.
G P F L H		New Romney & Littlestone-on-Sea	Kent	Southern (S.E.C.) / R.H.&D.	Branch—Lydd and Dungeness. / Terminus.
G P	3 0	New Ross, Vale Brick & Tile Wharf	Staffs	L.M.S.(N.S.)	Chesterton.
G P		New Ross	Kilkenny	L.M.S.(D.S.E.)	Macmine Junction and Waterford.
		New Rufford Colliery	Notts	G.W.(Mid.)	See Bolsover Col. Co. (Blidworth).
		NEW—	Down		
		(Station)	Down	B.&Newry	Adjoining G. N. (I.) Station.
G	2 0	Albert Basin	Down	G.N.(I.)	Branch from King Street Junction.
G	1 10	Bridge Street Junction	Armagh	D.N.&G.–G.N.(I.)	Bridge Street Junction and Greenore.
		Carrick Bros. Siding	Armagh	D.N.&G.	Edward Street and Greenore.
G		Dublin Bridge	Down	G.N.(I.)	Edward Street and Dublin Bridge.
G P F L H C	5 0	Edward Street (G.N. (I.))	Down	{G.N.(I.)} / {D.N.&G.}	Gorngh Wood and Warrenpoint. / Over G. N. (I.) from Bridge Str. Jn.
P		Newseat	Aberdeen	L.N.E.(G.N. of S.)	Maud and Peterhead.

EXPLANATIONS—G Goods Station. P Passenger and Parcel Station. P* Passenger, but not Parcel or Miscellaneous Traffic.
F Furniture Vans, Carriages, Portable Engines, and Machines on Wheels. L Live Stock.
H Horse Boxes and Prize Cattle Vans. C Carriages by Passenger Train.

Extracts from the Railway Clearing House (RCH) *Hand-book of Railway Stations,* circa 1929, showing the vast number of private and company wharves and sidings in and around the docks at Newport. *Courtesy Mr D. C. Sims, Newport Harbour Commissioners Office*

3.
THE TOWN DOCK

The Town Dock, or Old Dock as it was generally known, was situated in the town of Newport, a mile or so up the River Usk from the Alexandra Docks. Authorised by an Act of 1835, it was opened for trade on 10 October 1842, at a cost of £195,000. An extension under the Newport Dock Company Act of 1854 was completed and opened on 2 March 1858. These docks became the oldest property of the Alexandra (Newport & South Wales) Docks & Railway Company on 1 January 1884.

As in the case of the Alexandra North and South Docks, one side of the docks was devoted to coal shipping, while the other handled imports and general exports. The total area covered by the docks was 11½ acres, with the total length of 1,753 feet and a width of some 300 feet. The depth of water was about 5 feet less than the Alexandra Docks.

The trade from the Town Dock was mainly in timber, with the whole of one end laid out as a timber slipway.

Map of the Old, or Town, Dock at Newport, November 1907. *Cardiff Public Library*

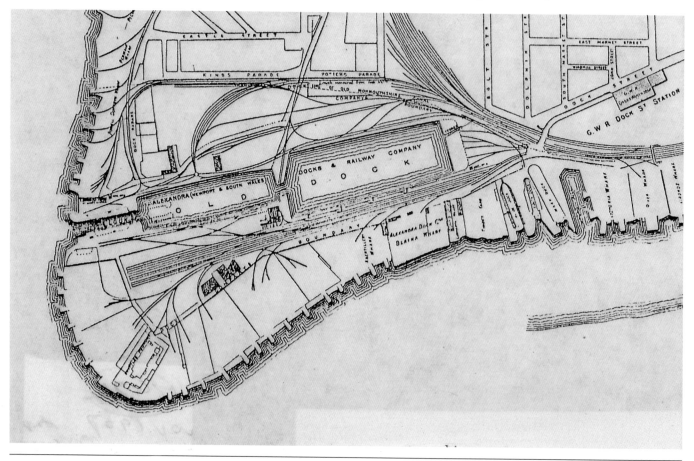

Other shipments consisted of grain, hay and potatoes; this type of cargo suited the various types of smaller vessels that used these docks; the cargo was worked aboard by the crews themselves.

The first dock to be entered, that opened in 1842, was known as the Outer Basin, and covered an area of 4 acres. For 12 years this dock met the requirements of the town, before the 7½-acre extension of 1858 was opened; this was badly needed as annual shipments had risen to 250,000 tons and were rising steadily. The extension was named the Inner Basin. Designed by Mr Abernethy MInstCE and constructed by the firm of Messrs Rennie & Logan at a cost of £64,000, it was 1,000 feet in length and 400 feet wide.

The Town Dock boasted an assortment of hydraulic cranes. Number 1, on the east side, was of the movable type with a fixed jib and a lifting capacity of 30 cwt, while on the west side was crane number 2; this was of the fixed type, and capable of lifting a maximum of 25 cwt. At the junction of the Inner Basin was crane number 3, again a fixed type with a maximum lift of 25 cwt. Crane number 4 was located on the west side of the Inner Basin, and was fixed with a lifting capacity also of 25 cwt. Number 5 was a movable crane, also with a lifting capacity of 25 cwt, and finally there was number 6, of the fixed type but with a lifting capacity of 30 cwt.

The Hydraulic Generating Power Station that served the Town Dock was finally abandoned in 1902, when hydraulic power was supplied via one of the three power stations at the Alexandra North Dock. By 1904 plans were being laid to reduce these three power stations to one, which would have the generating capacity of all three; this was to be situated at the north end of the North Dock.

By 1914 the Town Dock was equipped with four coal hoists, three being made out of steel and having a lift of 35 feet above quay level. These were designed to deal with loaded coal wagons of 23 tons gross weight.

The Town Dock was finally closed in October 1930. The *GWR Magazine* of 1939 stated that 'The work in connection with the diversion of the Town Dock Feeder to the Alexandra Docks has been completed, and the water has been diverted. The old feeder, which passed under part of the town, has been filled in with sand to prevent collapse. The filling in of the Outer Basin has commenced, a stone block dam having been constructed across the entrance.'

Today all trace of the Town Dock has disappeared. The site was filled in and built upon, and a modern shopping complex and bus terminus now cover the former docks.

The Blaina Wharf

This wharf, which adjoined the Town Dock, was also taken over by the ANDR in 1884. By 1904 it accommodated three hydraulic cranes with a lifting capacity of 2 tons, ideally suited for vessels built to carry 3,000-ton cargoes. Up to 1904 this wharf was notable in its handling of iron ore, which was discharged here en route to the furnaces of South Wales, usually the Blaenavon works.

A sketch drawn by Mr J. F. Mullock circa 1842 showing Newport's Town Dock, with St Woolos Church in the far distance. On the day of opening the vessels along the wharves were decked in streams of bunting, and flags were hung across the streets from public as well as private buildings in the town. *Associated British Ports*

The Entrance Lock that led into the Town Dock was 220 feet long and 61 feet wide; the depth of water to the entrance gates was 31 feet during average spring tides, reaching a depth of 36 feet during extraordinary spring tides. This early photograph, taken circa 1872 from the River Usk, shows the lock on the left, while on the extreme right is Penners Wharf. *Associated British Ports*

This scene shows the Outer Dock in 1910, with vessels in the background at anchor in the Inner Basin. It was at these docks, up to 1904, that the short-wheelbase 0-4-0 engines *Active*, *Alexandra* and *Trojan* worked. *ANDR booklet of 1916, Newport Harbour Commissioners Office*

The Monmouthshire Railway & Canal Company yard at the Town Dock, circa 1872. The sailing vessels were known as 'luggers', and were used for coastal trading between Newport and Bristol. *Associated British Ports*

Right A captured German submarine, *UB91*, at anchor at the north end of the Inner Basin during an inspection by Naval officers from the Admiralty circa 1916. Shortly after this visit the submarine was put on open display to the public, and a notice placed on the shed on the right stated that admission was 1 shilling. *Associated British Ports*

Below A view of the Inner Basin circa 1917, photographed from the lock gates that separated the Inner and Outer docks. On the right is one of the steam coastal vessels of the type that made frequent use of these docks. *Associated British Ports*

4.
THE PC&N:
PONTYPRIDD TO PENRHOS

Almost all of the railway companies that operated in South Wales had their own marked individuality and variety, and the PC&N line was no different. The following photographs show a varied selection of the types of engines used, the coaching stock, most of which was second-hand, and the closeness of part of the line to the Glamorganshire Canal, providing a rather picturesque setting. Variety was also provided by the other independent railway companies that came into daily contact with the PC&N as it travelled onwards towards its goal, the ANDR's Alexandra Docks complex.

The need for an independent line of railway was urgently discussed between Sir George Elliot and Lord Tredegar during the Alexandra Docks Company's board meeting on 16 July 1877. The conclusion was that a short line running between the town of Pontypridd and Caerphilly was needed as a connecting link to give the town of Newport and the Alexandra Docks direct and independent communication with the valleys of Aberdare and the Rhondda; also, the increase in coal traffic via the Tredegar Park Mile into the docks would increase the profits and royalties paid to Lord Tredegar and the other shareholders.

During the remaining part of 1877 Mr David Davies, MP and colliery owner, offered financial help with the building of the line, but later withdrew his offer. Perhaps he had other matters on his mind - the building of a railway line to the town of Barry, maybe.

On 29 November, on behalf of the ANDR, Mr Parkinson held a series of public meetings in the districts that would be affected by the proposed new railway line. The full reports that appeared in all the local newspapers must have caused quite a stir. It had been decided that land would have to be purchased of sufficient width to allow for the building of a double line, and not a single line as was at first thought.

Mr Parkinson had already reported to the board on 20 June that the earnings of the Alexandra Docks had shown a gratifying increase from the year before. However, a careful analysis by Sir George Elliot convinced not only himself but also the board that until the railway rates between the South Wales coalfields and Newport were made equal with the rates of those coalfields and Cardiff, the earnings of the Alexandra Docks would only be made secure if the coal traffic from the South Wales coalfields went to Newport via the proposed Pontypridd and Caerphilly railway line into the Alexandra Docks.

Thus the Pontypridd, Caerphilly & Newport Railway Company was born, incorporated by an Act of Parliament on 8 August 1878. Engineered by Mr J. W. Szlumper, the line was double-tracked as far as the Rhymney connection.

The line opened to coal traffic on 7 July 1884. The coal trains were manned 'with agreement' by the drivers and staff of the Taff Vale Railway from that date, until the agreement was discontinued, at the TVR's request, some 22 years later.

As fortune would have it, at that time the Mersey Railway Company had some unwanted engines for sale, and as the ANDR wanted to replace the original engines that had been used by the TVR on the coal traffic, ten were purchased for use on the coal trains from the Rhondda to Newport Docks, but this time operated by ANDR crews. This situation came into effect from 30 April 1906 and lasted until the railway grouping Act of 1922 came into force, when all trains were handled by the newly re-formed Great Western Railway (often using the same men).

The through passenger service started on 28 December 1887 with three trains each way, based at Pontypridd and running from the town's TVR station direct to Newport. This service was worked entirely by the staff of the ANDR until 1 January 1899, when agreement was reached for GWR staff to take over the through services, which in 1892 had increased to four trains each way, worked from Newport.

On 1 September 1904 the ANDR took over the local passenger service, running from its own Pontypridd Tram Road Halt to the Rhymney Railway's Caerphilly station. Following a review, from 1 January 1917, during the First World War period, the service was extended to run into the Brecon & Merthyr's station at Machen, where connections were made with the B&M trains to Newport.

The passenger service usually consisted of a 'push-pull'-fitted engine with one or two coaches, or one of the 'local' service railmotor sets, which had been introduced in September 1904. They were crewed by ANDR staff until 1922, when the line became part of the GWR group.

The ANDR acquired the PC&N by an Act of Parliament of 6 August 1897, but it was not until 31 December that the staff of the ANDR actually took over the general duties on the line. Although the board of directors of the ANDR had instigated the birth of the PC&N for their benefit, for tax and capital investment purposes the PC&N remained a separate railway company.

Below The line under construction - an extract from the *Pontypridd Observer*, 18 June 1881. *Pontypridd Public Library*

Right The railway is complete, and an arrangement reached with the Taff Vale - an extract from the *Pontypridd Chronicle*, 16 August 1884. *Pontypridd Public Library*

Below right Last-minute delay - an extract from the *Pontypridd Chronicle* of 26 January 1884. *Pontypridd Public Library*

NEW RAILWAYS.—The operations in connection with the line from Pontypridd to Newport via Caerphilly are being carried out with the utmost vigour, under the conductorship of Mr Mackay, Newport, Mon. At a spot midway between here and Treforest on the Pentrebach road, a small mountain of hard stone is being removed by means of the powder blasting process, and men are employed day and night to hasten its completion, the stone produced being intended for the construction of a viaduct of several spans to cross the river Taff. Behind the Glyntaff church and vicarage at the other side of this large amount of stone and where the "navvies" are comparatively uninterrupted owing to the ground being level and loamy. Most marked progress has been made and we may hope to hear of this excellent enterprise being completed in a very short time, and then the inhabitants of the Rhondda Valley and Pontypridd will no longer have to submit to the tedious journey of going to Cardiff *en route* for Newport and the North.—The Clydach Valley from Glyncoch farm to Ynysybwl is alive with the sounds of the "navvies'" implements, and already a road whereon the outcome of the Stephenson's modest invention may be allowed to have its run, has made its appearance, of course the line is not completed, nor are the pits sunk at Ynysybwl yet, but these are things we are earnestly looking forward to, although at the sacrifice of so pretty a valley, that Lord Aberdare was once heard to say, "It is the prettiest I have seen." But commerce and trade override all things, and we hope this will help to stimulate to no considerable degree the wealth and industry of Pontypridd and district.

THE PONTYPRIDD CAERPHILLY AND NEWPORT RAILWAY.

The half-yearly meeting of the shareholders of this company was held on Friday, at 60, Gracechurch-street, London, near the chairmanship of Mr C. J. Parkinson, managing director.—The Chairman in moving the adoption of the report said he had great pleasure in informing them that since their last meeting their railway had been completed, and was now in perfect working order, with a double line of rails, capable of carrying any amount of traffic capable of being shipped at Newport. But from causes of a temporary and evanescent character, there has been some annoying obstruction at the Basseleg end of their railway. This had brought out clearly the wisdom of the course adopted last year, when Parliament, in spite of a determined and powerful opposition, granted this company powers for continuing their line direct to the Alexandra Docks, thus giving Newport an independent access to the great coalfields of South Wales. This new portion of their railway and the necessary sidings and adjuncts in connection therewith were in course of construction, and were capable of being completed early in the ensuing year. By these means, and by virtue of an important working agreement with the Taff Vale Railway, which had been entered into for a long period of years, Newport had been made practically part of the Taff Vale Railway system, giving that efficient line an additional port, and providing independent and unfettered access to and from Newport from the Rhondda and all other valleys on the Taff Vale system. This arrangement was of incalculable importance to the colliery owners and freighters, as it would, they believed, place Newport, with its easy and safe access and unrivalled shipping facilities, on as favourable terms for export and import to and from the Rhondda and other valleys as any other port or harbour in the Bristol Channel.—Mr J. S. Adams seconded the motion, which was carried unanimously, and the proceedings closed with a vote of thanks to the chairman.

PONTYPRIDD, CAERPHILLY, AND NEWPORT RAILWAY.

It was hoped that this railway would have been opened for traffic at the commencement of this month. Owing, however, to a defect in one of the abutments of the bridge crossing the River Taff at Pontypridd, men re pulling it down and propping the girders with timber, so that many months must now elapse before the re-construction will be completed.

THE WORKING OF THE PONTYPRIDD AND CAERPHILLY RAILWAY.

AGREEMENT BETWEEN THE TAFF VALE RAILWAY COMPANY AND SIR G. ELLIOT.

On Friday, Sir George Elliot informed the Parliamentary Committee inquiring into the Barry Dock Railway Bill that he and Mr Inskip, the Chairman of the Taff Vale Railway Company had that day signed an agreement by which the Pontypridd, Caerphilly, and Newport line would be worked by the Taff Vale people. He denied that it was an attempt to throw dust into the eyes of the Committee, but a definite arrangement come to, so that the Taff Vale Company would have an alternate route to Cardiff (by means of the Pontypridd Company's running powers over the Rhymney line) and the Rhondda colliery proprietors would have a way to Newport Docks. The following is the text of the agreement :—" Heads of arrangement made the 20th day of June, 1884, between the Taff Vale Railway Company (hereinafter called the Taff company) of the one part, and the Pontypridd, Caerphilly, and Newport Railway Company (hereinafter called the Pontypridd Company). (1) Upon the opening of the Pontypridd Company's railways for such goods and mineral traffic as hereinafter mentioned, the Taff Vale Railway Company with, so far as they lawfully can, having regard to the existing rights of the other companies or persons, provide locomotive power and work from the Pontypridd Junction south of Pontypridd all goods and mineral traffic passing from the Taff Vale Railway to the Pontypridd, Caerphilly, and Newport Railway at Pontypridd Junction, and consigned to and destined for Newport and places beyond; to interchange sidings at or near the junction of the Pontypridd Company's railway and the Alexandra Dock Company's railway, and will also provide locomotive power, and work to Pontypridd Junction all goods and mineral traffic over the Pontypridd Company's railway, and consigned to places on the Taff Company's system, or any intermediate place between the same interchange sidings and Pontypridd. (2) The Taff Vale Company shall not be required to convey from Pontypridd Junction to the said interchange sidings laden trucks of less than 26 wagons or trucks, or to make more than two shunts thereof at the interchange sidings, which shall at all times be kept clear from the reception of such laden traffic. (3) The Taff Vale Company shall convey the return empties from the said sidings in fair average trains, but the return empties shall be properly sorted and placed ready for their several destinations by the Pontypridd Company. (4) The railways over which the Taff Vale Company shall be required to convey traffic in pursuance of these heads of agreement, shall be provided with all necessary sidings, signals, junctions, and other conveniences, and the said railways, signals, sidings, junctions, and other conveniences shall be maintained in good and sufficient working order by the Pontypridd Company, who shall erect and maintain, and keep and supply a sufficient water tank at a convenient place at the interchange sidings, and the Taff Vale Company's engineer shall be supplied with water therefrom free of cost. The Pontypridd Railway Company shall pay and discharge all road tolls, sidings, and other charges payable in respect of any traffic which shall be worked by the Taff Vale Company under this agreement, and shall provide any extra engine power required for taking traffic up the Machen incline. (6) The Taff Company shall, in respect of coal and coke conveyed by them between the junction at Pontypridd of the Taff Vale Company and the Pontypridd, Caerphilly, and Newport Railway, and the junction east of Caerphilly of the Rhymney Company, and the Brecon and Merthyr Tydvil Junction Railway, and between the Brecon and Merthyr Junction Railway and the Alexandra Dock sidings, be paid by the Pontypridd Company one farthing per ton per mile, and in like proportion for a less distance, and for other goods such sum as in default of agreement shall be from time to time fixed by an arbitrator appointed by the Board of Trade on the application of either party hereto, with the usual clearing-house allowances. The Taff Vale Company shall also in respect of coal and coke traffic conveyed by them between the said junction east of Caerphilly and the said interchange be paid by the Pontypridd Company 24·100d (twenty-four one-hundredths of a penny) per ton per mile and in like proportion for a less distance, and for other goods, such sum as in default of agreement shall be from time to time fixed by an arbitrator, appointed by the Board of Trade, on the application of either party, with the usual clearing-house allowances. (7) All-through rates for goods carried to the Taff Vale Company's system over the line of the Pontypridd Company shall be subject to the consent of the Taff Vale Company, or an arbitrator under this agreement. (8) Payment to be made monthly by the Pontypridd Company, and that company to settle with other companies. (9) Signalmen, stores, and all costs of sidings and junction expenses at and between Pontypridd Junction and the said interchange sidings to be provided by and at the expense of the Pontypridd Company. (10) Until the completion and opening for traffic of the Pontypridd Company's authorised railway between the Brecon and Merthyr Tydvil Junction Railway and the Alexandra Dock sidings, the Taff Company shall work, on the terms before mentioned, the traffic referred to between the said Pontypridd Junction and interchange sidings at Bassaleg to be provided by the Pontypridd Company. (11) Except as herein expressly provided, nothing in this agreement shall affect any of the existing agreements between the companies or any provision in force in favour of the company. (12) Any dispute between the parties hereto not provided for shall be settled in accordance with the provisions of the Railway Companies Arbitration Act, 1859. (13) This agreement to remain in force for ten years from the 1st July, 1884, and to be afterwards subject to six months' notice on either side. (14) A formal agreement embodying the above terms to be settled between the parties by Mr Phipton Beale, or, in failing by some counsel to be named by the Attorney-General, who shall have power to add such other provisions as he shall think expedient for carrying out the intention of the parties hereto as herein expressed For the Taff Vale Railway Company, James Inskip, chairman. For the Pontypridd, Caerphilly, and Newport Railway, George Elliot."

Report on the PC&N/TVR agreement in the *Pontypridd Chronicle*, 28 June 1884. *Pontypridd Public Library*

22

When descending the main and other severe inclines the Driver must give 1 crow to stop putting Brakes down and 2 crows to lift Brakes when too many are applied.

SPECIAL INSTRUCTIONS TO ENGINEMEN AND SIGNALMEN.

UP TRAINS.—Up Rhondda Trains, having no work to do short of Pontypridd Junction, when approaching Treforest North must give **one crow**. The signalman must give **1-2** on the bell for the line upon which the train is travelling to P. C. and N. Junction immediately after sending "Train on Line," so that when P. C. and N. Junction asks "**Is line clear**" of Pontypridd Junction he may use the "**Is line clear for Branch Goods**" code.

Up Trains having work to do at Pontypridd Station, New Warehouse, or Pontshon Norton, or requiring to stop at Pontypridd for Water, must give three short whistles twice, thus /// pause /// when approaching Treforest North, and the signalman there must, immediately after sending "Train on Line," give **1-2-1** on the Bell for the line on which the Train is travelling to P. C. and N. Junction, where the train will be dealt with as may be expedient.

DOWN TRAINS.—The following engine whistles must be given at :—

Gyfeillon Lower, if they have no work to do at Coke Ovens.

Rhondda Cutting Junction, after completing work at Coke Ovens.

Pontshon Norton, if they have no work to do at Pontypridd Warehouse.

Pontypridd Northern, after completing work at Pontypridd Warehouse.

By Trains proceeding to P. C. and N.—**3 long and 1 crow.**

By Trains proceeding to No. 2—**2 long.**

The signalman at the respective cabins, on hearing the whistles named, must immediately after sending "Train on Line," send the bell signals (shown on page 23) to the signal cabin in advance, and when sent from Gyfeillon Lower or Pontshon Norton, must be transmitted to Pontypridd Junction to enable Pontypridd Junction (for Trains going to P. C. and N., when asking "**Is Line Clear**" of P. C. and N. Junction) to use the Code "**Is Line Clear for Branch Goods**"; or (for Trains going to No. 2 Down Road, after asking P. C. and N. Junction "Is Line Clear for Ordinary Goods or Mineral Train") to send the specified Bell Code forward.

23

The Bell Codes are :—

Trains to P. C. and N. ... ... **1-2.**

" No. 2 Down ... ... **1-2-1.**

The Drivers of through Trains proceeding to any Branch on approaching the Signal Cabin next but one before reaching the Junction, must sound the standard whistle according to the Line they are on, and the Signalman must immediately after sending "Train on Line" give **3-5** to the Signal Cabin in advance, to enable the Signal Cabin in the rear of the Junction to ask "**Is Line Clear for Branch Goods**" of the Junction Signal Cabin.

The Driver of a through Train that may require to pass from one road to another through a facing shunt, must at the second Signal Cabin next but one to that having control of the shunt (or the next one to it, if circumstances such as having to do work at intermediate Sidings should render it necessary), sound the standard whistle according to the Line on which he is running, and the Signalman on hearing it must immediately after sending "Train on Line" give the following Codes on the Bell for the Line on which the Train is travelling, to the Signal Cabin in advance :—

From No. 1 to No. 2 Road **2-5**

" No. 2 " 1 " **5-2**

to enable the Signalman where the change is required to be made, to ask and obtain "Line Clear" from the Signal Cabin in advance for the Line upon which the Train requires to proceed.

SPECIAL WHISTLES.
Main Lines (Con.)

STATIONS AND JUNCTIONS.	TO AND FROM	WHISTLES.	REMARKS.
P. C. & N. Junction ...	Old Warehouse Siding...	4 short	
Pontypridd Junction ...	Rhondda Branch	3	
	Chapel Siding	1 crow	
	Down Branch and Bay...	2	
	Up " "	2 and 1 short	
	Penrhiew Siding	1 crow and 1 short	
	Down Main and Down Branch ...	4 short	
	Crawshay's Sidings and Bay	1 crow and 2 short	

Extracts from the Taff Vale Railway Company Rule Book of 1894, regarding working on the PC&N line. *Courtesy Mr D. G. Thomas*

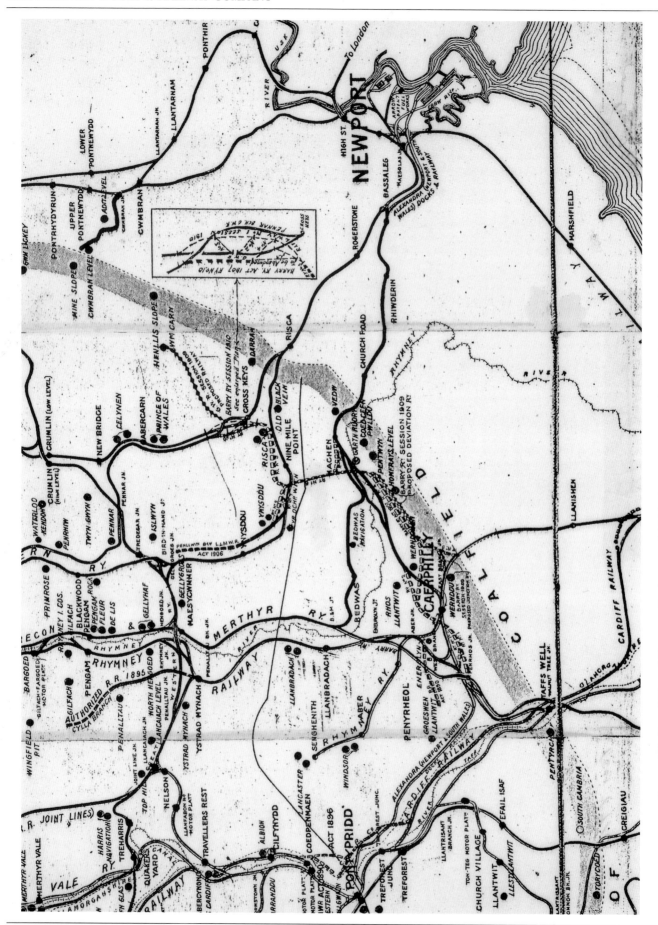

Pontypridd, Caerphilly and Newport district map of 1910, showing existing railways and proposed deviations. *Courtesy Alan Powell*

Right The PC&N junction was located at the southern end of Pontypridd station, 16 chains from the PC&N's Interchange Sidings West signal box, and opened on 7 July 1884 for the handling of mineral traffic. This photograph, dated 13 July 1958, shows the PC&N line from PCN Junction, facing towards Treforest TVR station; the junction can be seen just past the platform water pump, heading off to the left and crossing the PCN Tramroad bridge in the centre of the photograph. Further left can be seen the PC&N viaduct that crossed the River Taff and carried the line towards Glyntaff. The signal box is PCN Junction.

Originally trains from Caerphilly ran into the TVR's Pontypridd station via PCN Junction, but the ANDR was not prepared to pay the TVR's extra charges for the use of the junction or station, so subsequently the services terminated at Tram Road Halt. Because there was no crossover there, the return train had to be propelled for 400 yards 'wrong line' to the crossover at the PCN's Interchange Sidings signal box near Glyntaff Halt, where it could be crossed on to the correct line. This section of the PC&N from PCN Junction to the Glyntaff Interchange Sidings ground frame closed to all traffic on 31 July 1967. *J. J. Davis*

Below A closer, and rather picturesque, view of the PC&N junction in 1952, the line branching off the former TVR Cardiff and Merthyr main line and passing over the Broadway, which was formerly known as the Tramroad; the light engine seen here is approx- imately where the PC&N's Tram Road Halt was located. In the background can be seen the vast area that was known as the Interchange Sidings, while Glyntaff Halt was situated at the base of the cliffs in the distance.

Today the new Pontypridd bypass is almost completed, and runs along the former PC&N route from Interchange Sidings to the Broadway. *R. Wilding, courtesy D. J. Rees*

Right Pontypridd Tram Road Halt was opened on 1 September 1904 for local passenger services. It was on that date that the Board of Trade inspected and passed the arrangements made for what was then classed as a 'motor car service' between Pontypridd and Caerphilly. The Board's report stated that the Halt consisted of a ground platform, ie wooden planks placed side by side, very cheap and effective (that is until they got wet and slippery), and that this platform was on the up side only, with both up and down passengers using it. The report also stated that this and the other new platforms were to be provided with a lamp at the entrance barrier of the footpath approaches, and that these barriers were to be opened by the conductors on the arrival of the cars.

On 28 April 1906 Lt-Col E. Druitt RE reported to the Board of Trade that he had inspected the new motor car platform, ie the rebuilt Tram Road Halt. He stated that the old car platform at rail level had been replaced by one 100 feet long by 10 feet wide, and 3 ft 6 ins above rail level, and that the old shelter has been extended, with a ladies' waiting room with conveniences added, and additional lighting provided. The platform was reached by a ramp, well fenced and closed by a gate, and access could only be gained to the platform when a motor car was about to leave. New signalling at the Halt meant that the old arrangement of working wrong line was abolished from 1 May 1906; a new signal box, Interchange Sidings West, was provided at the far end of the river bridge in the Glyntaff direction.

This photograph shows the rebuilt Tram Road Halt, which opened on 1 May 1906, looking towards the TVR's Pontypridd station in June 1921; the Halt was closed entirely by the Great Western Railway Company on 10 July 1922, just over a year later. *D. K. Jones*

Below The PC&N viaduct spanning the River Taff at Pontypridd, situated a few yards from Tram Road Halt, photographed on 29 June 1963.

In June 1986 the piers of the viaduct and the site of the former Tram Road Halt were demolished to make a car park. Today the trackbed from Interchange Sidings to the abutments of the PC&N Tram Road bridge, which for many years was left for nature to reclaim, has gone, and is now to form part of the new relief road that will bypass Pontypridd. *Courtesy J. J. Davis*

The firm of Brown, Lenox of Pontypridd, originally known as the Newbridge Anchor & Chain Works, was first awarded Admiralty contracts in 1808. Following the signing of a formal contract between the firm and the PC&N on 14 November 1907, a siding was provided at the works for the transportation of forgings and castings by the PC&N to the ANDR docks at Newport. This photograph circa 1910 shows a general view of the Brown, Lenox Works next to the Glamorgan Canal. The PC&N line was situated at the far end of the works and can be glimpsed going off towards the trees in the top left-hand corner. *Pontypridd Public Library*

BROWN, LENOX & CO., LTD.

Admiralty Contractors for over 100 Years.

Pontypridd and London.

MANUFACTURERS OF

Chain Cables, Buoys, Moorings & Anchors.

Supply all the principal Harbours and Docks in the World with Buoys and Moorings, and have supplied NEWPORT with all the Buoys and Moorings for the Dock now being opened, and those at present in use.

A Brown, Lenox & Co Ltd advertisement circa 1914. *ANDR booklet of 1914, Newport Harbour Commissioners Office*

This photograph taken circa 1906 in the Brown, Lenox Works shows one of the GWR open plank wagons used by the PC&N, in this case one of the four-plank examples of 10 tons tare. The chain links on display here were part of a shipment that was en route to the Cunard Steam Ship Company, bound for their vessel the *Aquitania* then at anchor in the River Mersey. *Messrs Brown, Lenox & Co*

An inside view of the works circa 1910. In 1858 Isambard Kingdom Brunel visited here to purchase chains for his ship, the all-metal PSS *Great Eastern*, a steamship that was six times longer than any ship afloat at the time. The well-known photograph of him being 'hung in chains' was taken during that visit. *Messrs Brown, Lenox & Co*

ANDR engine No 14, formerly GWR No 1426, with driver Owen Morgan and fireman Garnet Lang in a photograph taken circa 1919 at Glyntaff after she had a received a new boiler at Hawthorn Leslie's works in December 1919. This '517' Class engine was one of two permanently shedded at Glyntaff shed. *Welsh Industrial & Maritime Museum, Cardiff*

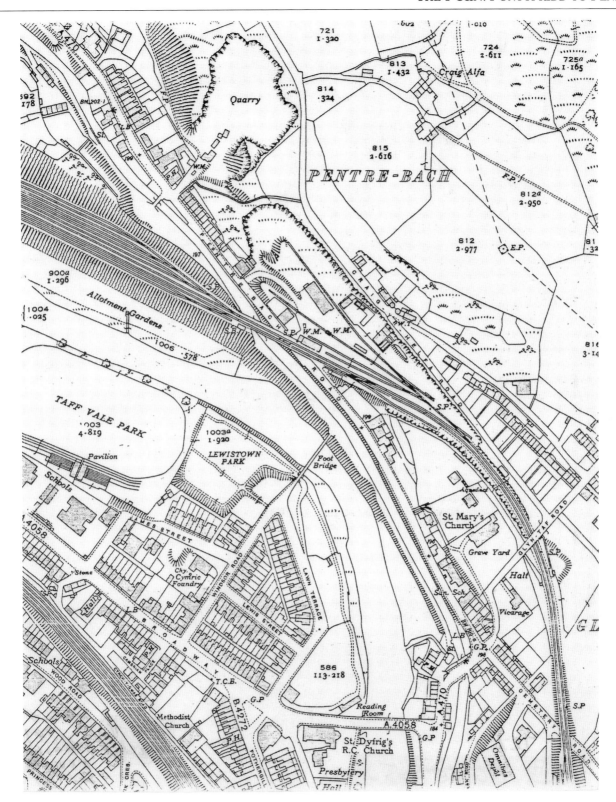

Part of an Ordnance Survey map showing the Interchange Sidings (top left), Glyntaff Halt (centre, where the line crosses Pentrebach Road) and Treforest Halt (below right). Interchange Sidings were some 30 chains in length with signal boxes situated at the east and west ends, and were used for the marshalling and interchange of all types of traffic. By 1904 there was also a considerable amount of general trade being handled at the PC&N goods station at Glyntaff en route to and from the Alexandra Docks. However, in the GWR summer timetable of 1938 there was a paragraph that stated that the signal box was to be opened only as required, thus showing that trade had dropped quite a lot by then.

On 2 January 1967 the PC&N line from Interchange Sidings to Penrhos Junction, which by then was operated by a hand-operated ground frame located at the Interchange Sidings end, was closed and locked out of use permanently. *Reproduced from the 1943 Ordnance Survey map*

Above Glyntaff was opened on 1 September 1904. Later, after the Grouping, it was renamed Glyntaff Halt by the GWR on 1 July 1924. It closed to passenger services on 5 May 1932.

This postcard view circa 1910 shows the Halt on the extreme left, while in the centre foreground is the goods shed and railway bridge over the Pentrebach Road. The railway bridge in the extreme right-hand corner takes the line over the Glamorganshire Canal (see the map on the previous page). In 1906 the Glyntaff goods station's telephone number was '31 National', a far cry from the length of today's numbers! The postcard is captioned 'Treforest', which is the area beyond the halt; it was a locally issued card that was on sale in many of the shops in the town at that time.

Unfortunately the southern end of the site is out of sight; it was there that the engine shed was located, equipped with full engine and railmotor servicing facilities from 1 September 1904 until September 1922. In the ANDR Appendix of May 1906 instructions regarding the 'motor car services' stated that payments must be made to the Glyntaff agent.

Today all traces of the Halt have been erased by the A470 trunk road, which now covers the site. The goods depot has also gone and the site where it stood is now part of a warehouse and storage building. The shed area is now in a neglected state, overgrown and covered with brambles. Even the cutting that carried the line past St Mary's Church is impossible to follow due to being densely wooded. *Pontypridd Public Library*

General View, Treforest.

Left Another slightly broader postcard view of Treforest village, circa 1910. In the foreground is again Glyntaff Halt, and on the right-hand side part of the goods

GLYNTAF.

THE NEW RAILWAY BRIDGE.—The bridge erected on the road to Craig-yr-Haulfa village, over the Pontypridd and Caerphilly Railway, is, it appears at present, likely to result in an action at law being instituted by the owners of property in that village against the company, their plea being that the ascent to the bridge is so steep, without, as they allege, the slightest reason for it, as to make the village difficult of access, and thereby seriously depreciates the value of the houses in the locality. The ascent is so steep that vehicular traffic is almost impossible, and hauliers already decline to take fuel in carts to the scores of houses above the bridge.

An extract from the *Pontypridd Chronicle* of 6 August 1881. *Pontypridd Public Library*

shed. In the middle can be seen the goods siding and the Halt's waiting room. On the left is the Glamorganshire Canal, passing by Pontypridd Gasworks in the top left-hand corner; the gasworks also had a contract with the PC&N. The river is the River Taff.

The coaches in the foreground are the former Barnum & Bailey circus coaches. Also in view is one of the former Mersey Railway coaches, a four-wheeler Brake 3rd, which was purchased in September 1904.

In the Board of Trade recommendations of 1904 the Halt was to be of the ground platform type, but as can clearly be seen in this postcard it now has a raised platform. It is possible that this was done on 28 April 1906 when Tram Road Halt was similarly rebuilt. *Author's collection*

The shelters seen here are typical of the GWR's policy on spending money on this line, and one can see that no expense was spared! The sign beyond the fence reads 'GWR. Trespassers will be prosecuted'. The Halt closed on 17 September 1956, and today the site is covered by the extended playing field of the nearby comprehensive school. *The late Mr T. B. Sands, courtesy of Westrail Enterprises*

Below ANDR engine No 21 hauling logs on a Treforest to Caerphilly goods train, photographed near Treforest at the Gasworks Sidings. This 0-6-0 saddle tank engine was built by Messrs R. Stephenson, and renumbered by the GWR as 670. Photographed on 19 May 1919, it was withdrawn from service in 1926. *LCGB (Ken Nunn Collection)*

Above Treforest Halt on 9 June 1952, looking towards Rhydyfelin. Situated in a cutting with an overbridge next to it, Treforest opened on 1 September 1904 for local passenger services; it was renamed by the GWR as Treforest Halt on 1 July 1924.

TREFOREST.

A MAN IN THE CANAL.—One of the "navvies" engaged on the Pontypridd and Caerphilly Railway here, had a narrow escape from drowning in the canal the other night, he was rescued by the proprietor of the Llanbradach Arms, who brought him to the bank by the hair of his head, owing to the darkness of the night the poor fellow must have missed his footing. There is a great public danger still existing along the Pentrebach road, in the form of unprotected openings in the wall bounding the canal.

An extract from the *Pontypridd Chronicle* of 25 June 1881. *Pontypridd Public Library*

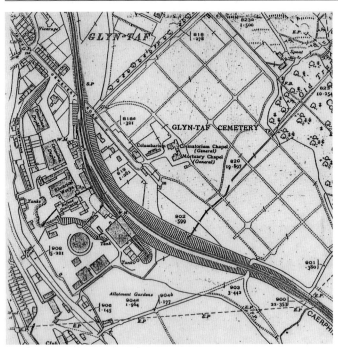

Left A map showing Pontypridd Gasworks and Sidings. On 10 December 1896 an agreement was signed with the ANDR to transport coal to the gasworks, which were in the control of the Pontypridd Urban District Council; a further agreement was signed with the GWR on 16 September 1926. The sidings were listed in the 1904 edition of the Railway Clearing House Handbook of Stations under the ANDR, but it is presumed that they were serviced by the TVR until 1906.

A Board of Trade report of 9 April 1908 concerning the sidings stated: 'I have inspected the new sidings at Gasworks Sidings, further interlocking is required and that the signal box there contains 13 working and one spare lever.' A ground frame, worked by the guards on the goods trains, was installed in 1931 for the working of the sidings on the up side of the line; these sidings were situated 588 yards from Interchange East signal box.

Today no trace is left of Gasworks Sidings. Even the impressive dressed stone building was demolished in October 1990, and a car park now covers the whole area. *Reproduced from the 1943 Ordnance Survey map*

Below Map showing the line from Glyntaff (top left-hand corner) to Dynea via Rhydyfelin. *Reproduced from the 1938 Ordnance Survey map*

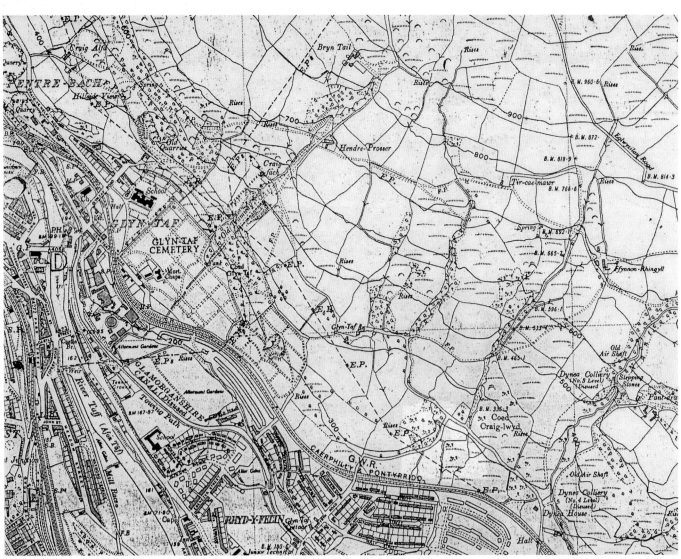

Above Rhydyfelin PC&N Halt was another of the stations opened on 1 September 1904 for local passenger services. The company even provided an occupational crossing for travellers to reach the down platform. Situated 1½ miles from Pontypridd, the station was renamed by the GWR in 1922 as Rhydyfelin High Level Halt, so as not to be confused with the nearby Halt of the former Cardiff Railway. According to *Clinker's Register* the Halt closed on 14 May 1928.

The Halt consisted of a sleeper-type wooden platform at ground level, and is seen here in June 1921 looking towards Dynea. A GWR locomotive is pulling a Barnum & Bailey coach and a converted railmotor trailer; the engine was on loan to the PC&N because the company's regular engine, No 14, was out of service. On the left can be seen one of the numerous cast iron notices, this one reading 'Beware of trains running in both directions when crossing'. *D. K. Jones*

Right This second Rhydyfelin Halt was opened by the GWR on 14 May 1928, 18 chains to the east of the PC&N facility; the Halt was thus a distance of 8 miles 79 chains from Machen Junction. It was this halt that was the cause of the destruction of autotrailer steps on forgetful occasions. It was the responsibility of the guard to ensure that the steps were raised or lowered on the approach to or when the leaving the halts along the line, but sometimes it was easier to leave them in place, especially as all of the PC&N halts were at ground level; however, this GWR-built halt was a raised platform type, and if the guard was new or forgetful the effect was dramatic, much to the amusement of his colleagues!

This photograph, taken on 27 August 1948, shows a passenger train on the Pontypridd to Caerphilly service pulled by former GWR 0-6-0PT No 6438; the leading trailer is of Rhymney Railway origin. It is interesting to note that while the platform seen on the left was of wooden construction, the other was of concrete. Note also the GWR corrugated tin shelter, which was typical of the type of shelter provided for the company's customers at these lower-classified halts. Rhydyfelin Halt closed on 8 June 1953, and today no trace can be seen of either station; the grey scar of the trackbed is now part of the Treforest to Nantgarw cycle track. *I. L. Wright*

Above Dynea was opened on 1 September 1904, and this photograph, taken in October 1908, shows the damage that resulted from heavy rain swelling the small stream above the halt and causing an avalanche of water and stones to flood the area, before overspilling into the nearby Glamorganshire Canal and causing a great deal more damage. The Halt can be seen up the path on the left, with workmen from the local authority clearing away the flood damage from the road running under the railway. Dynea was renamed by the GWR as Dynea Halt on 1 July 1924. Today no evidence of the Halt remains; like most of the facilities along this line, the buildings and wooden fencing have long gone, and even the soil that lay under the ballast has been removed to form a slipway from the track level to the base of the bridge foundations to form part of the new cycle track. *Courtesy of Starling Press*

Left This photograph shows Dynea Halt on 14 July 1956 looking somewhat the worse for wear just two months before closure, looking towards Upper Boat. A down siding, which was controlled by Dynea signal box, was located some 300 yards towards Upper Boat Halt, giving access to Dynea Colliery. This was added by the GWR in 1931, and at some later date a ground frame was installed, operated by the train guard. However, this siding must have been short-lived, as by 1943 the Ordnance Survey map shows no evidence of it. *R. M. Casserley*

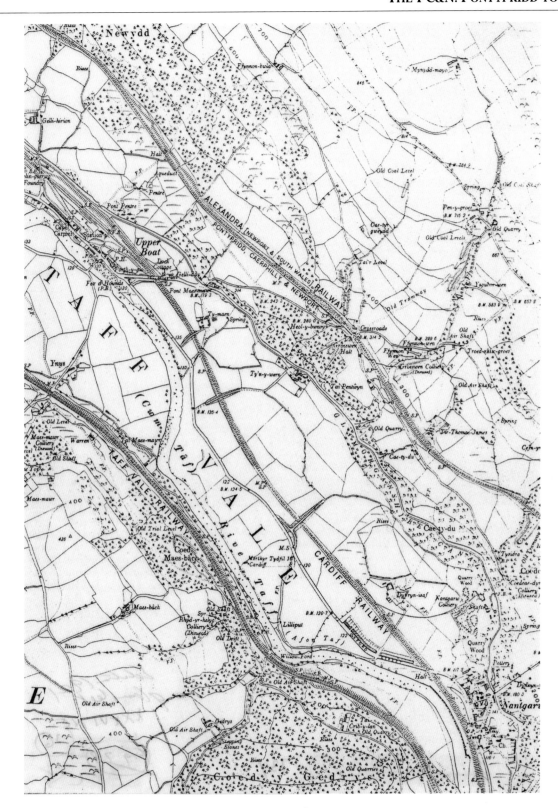

This map shows just how close the various railway lines were, and the competition for mineral and passenger traffic was a real battle before the GWR did some pruning.

Upper Boat, in the top left-hand corner, again opened on 1 September 1904 for local passenger services. The Board of Trade report stated that a foot overbridge had been provided to save passengers crossing the line to reach the down-side platform. It was renamed Upper Boat Halt by the GWR on 1 July 1924, and the GWR timetable for that year and again in 1926 shows it as a request stop only, and then only on certain passenger trains; it had not taken the GWR long to begin cutting back on parts of its newly acquired services. Upper Boat closed entirely to both goods and passenger services on 17 September 1956.

Groeswen Halt can be seen in the centre of the map, and Nantgarw at the bottom. *Reproduced from the 1921 Ordnance Survey map*

Above Groeswen station opened for local passenger services on 1 September 1904. After the Grouping, as with the other halts along this line, it was renamed by the GWR on 1 July 1924 as Groeswen Halt. This 1904 photograph looking towards Dynea shows the Halt, footpath and signal box all in a very tidy and clean state; it was possibly taken by the company photographer shortly after its opening to the public.

The house above the Halt at the end of the road bridge was the manager's house-cum-weighbridge for the tramroad leading from Groeswen Colliery to the siding at the Halt. *Pontypridd Public Library*

Left The site of Groeswen Halt seen from track level under the road bridge and looking in the opposite direction on 10 July 1958. The Halt had closed on 17 September 1956, and Groeswen Siding signal box (2 miles 63 chains from Interchange Sidings East) was demolished in the same year, but the water crane as well as the somewhat dilapidated fencing survive. In 1988 the trackbed was cleared and is also now part of the new cycle track, with a picnic area on the site of the Halt. The stone retaining wall behind the signal box remains, and is the only indication of where the Halt stood. *R. M. Casserley*

Above A slightly blurred photograph of ANDR engine No 14 with the 10.20 am Pontypridd to Caerphilly train, photographed near Nantgarw on 19 May 1919. *LCGB (Ken Nunn Collection)*

Below Nantgarw Halt was another of the stations opened for local passenger services on 1 September 1904, and was renamed Nantgarw High Level by the GWR on 1 July 1924; it closed entirely on 17 September 1956. This photograph, looking towards Groeswen on 4 September 1956, shows former GWR 0-6-0PT No 6411 arriving at the Halt with the 2.52 pm Pontypridd to Machen auto-train.

Today it is only by the use of old and new Ordnance Survey maps that it is possible to pinpoint the locations of these former halts. Most of them, including those at Groeswen and Nantgarw, were situated next to road bridges; these, some no wider than for a horse and cart to pass, are a good guide to their location. *S. Rickard*

NOTICE.

Alexandra (Newport & South Wales) Docks and Railway Company.

MOTOR CAR SERVICE

Commencing on JUNE 4th, 1911, a

SUNDAY SERVICE

Will be Run between

Pontypridd and Caerphilly

Calling at Intermediate Stations.

The Sunday Service will be provisional and experimental, and the Company do not bind themselves to the continuance thereof.

Full particulars of times and trains, see Company's Time Tables.

JOHN MACAULAY,

Newport, Mon., May, 1911. General Manager.

Left Another photograph of the auto-train service, now being propelled by No 6411, as it approaches Nantgarw Halt on its return journey to Pontypridd on 15 September 1956. This was rather a sad day, not only for the nearby residents that used this service, but also for railway enthusiasts, as it was the last day of the service between Pontypridd and Newport via Caerphilly before the final closure.

On 22 October 1987 the *Pontypridd Observer* reported that plans were to go ahead to convert part of the former PC&N line from Glyntaff Cemetery to Nantgarw Road into part of the Taff Valley Cycleway, and this is now in the latter stages of redevelopment. Credit must be given to the Taff Ely Council and the local Community Project members for making use of this former line, which over the years was beginning to revert to nature. *S. C. L. Phillips and D. K. Jones*

Left ANDR announcement of the 'Motor Car' Sunday service, *Pontypridd Observer*, 4 June 1911. *Pontypridd Public Library*

5.
THE RHYMNEY AND BRECON & MERTHYR: PENRHOS TO NEWPORT VIA CAERPHILLY

Penrhos Junction was the end of the PC&N line as such, and marked the start of the second phase of the journey, by running alongside the metals of the Rhymney Railway at first, then eventually joining them at Penrhos South Junction to head towards Caerphilly station via the level crossing at Watford Road and Caerphilly West Junction, a distance of some 5 miles 14 chains.

At this point mention of the complex arrangements needed to secure the PC&N's access to Alexandra Docks must be made. As mentioned earlier, on 8 August 1878 Parliament granted that the PC&N could run between a junction with the TVR at Pontypridd to a junction with the Rhymney Railway at Penrhos. By means of running powers granted to the PC&N it could then run over the B&M Caerphilly branch to Bassaleg, where it would join the former Monmouth Railway & Canal Company, by

now under the ownership of the GWR, and it was hoped that these powers would be sufficient to gain access to the ANDR lines at West Mendelgief Junction, Newport.

The Taff Vale Railway contracted to work the trains over the PC&N route to Newport Docks in the hope that this would lead to the PC&N becoming part of the TVR system. The first train of coal left Pontypridd on 7 July 1884, calling at Caerphilly station to pick up a Brecon & Merthyr pilot engine. However, on arrival at Bassaleg Junction the GWR declined to allow the PC&N train to pass over the junction.

After a couple of weeks of negotiations, the GWR gave way and the trains began to run into the Alexandra Docks in earnest on 25 July. Needless to say neither the Alexandra Docks nor the PC&N became part of the Taff Vale Railway.

The junction at Penrhos was governed by Penrhos North Junction signal box; this was responsible for directing traffic not only for the PC&N and Rhymney Railway, but also the Barry Railway.

This rather detailed photograph, looking west on 6 September 1956, shows Penrhos North Junction signal box, of GWR design. The train that can be seen in the distance on the right is the auto-train set for Pontypridd being propelled by engine No 6411 along the PC&N line. On the left is a goods train on the Barry Railway spur, which was built by the GWR to provide a link between the Rhymney Railway line (the centre pair of tracks) and the Barry Railway, which once crossed the junction on the viaduct the remains of which can be seen.

Alas, today only the viaduct piers and road bridge remain; the Rhymney line down the 'big bank' is a cycle track stretching from Taffs Well to Caerphilly, with fragments of ballast poking out from beneath the grass that has started to cover the area.
S. C. L. Phillips and D. K. Jones

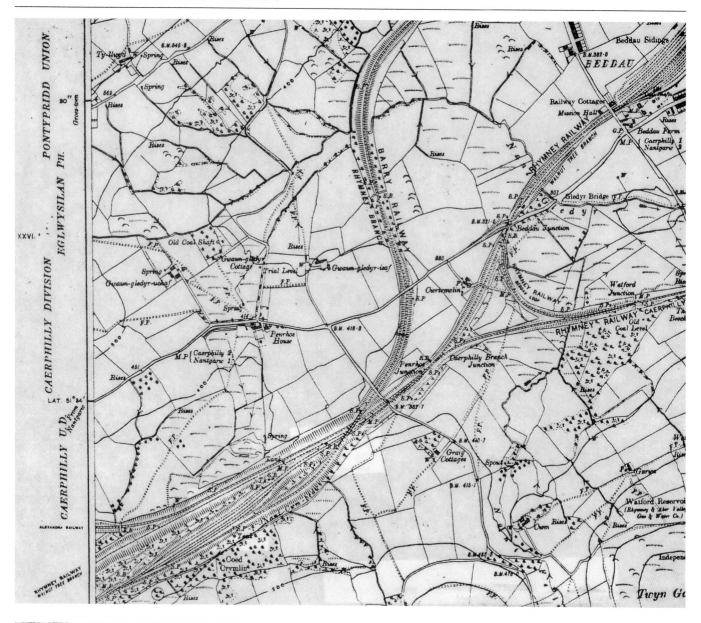

Above Penrhos Junction. In the bottom left-hand corner of the map the PC&N, Rhymney and Barry lines head off to Pontypridd, Taffs Well and Barry respectively. *Reproduced from the 1921 Ordnance Survey map*

Left Photographed from Penrhos Junction signal box on 6 September 1956, an auto-train trailer pulled by a former GWR pannier tank passes under the stone-built overbridge en route to Caerphilly, via the line that can be seen branching off to the right in the distance. *S. C. L. Phillips and D. K. Jones*

Right The section of the Rhymney Railway's line through Caerphilly to Machen was opened in 1867. For a short period the PC&N had its own platform at Caerphilly, shown in this old and rather faded photograph dating from about 1900, before the reconstruction of the station in 1914. This platform was situated on the Penrhos Junction side of the Caerphilly Road bridge, below St Martins Church, passengers obtaining their tickets from the Caerphilly station booking office. Photographed in winter time, the snow gives a clear edge to the path leading from the road to the platform. The remainder of the Rhymney Railway station can be seen under the road bridge.

From 1 April 1908 all PC&N traffic over Rhymney metals was operated with the assistance of Rhymney staff, then on 1 January 1917 the service between Caerphilly and Machen was extended to connect with the Brecon & Merthyr Railway's trains that ran to and from Newport station by using the Rhymney Railway's Senghenydd branch railmotor; this service lasted for a short period only, ceasing on 5 May 1919.

Today the Brecon & Merthyr Railway junction, formerly known as Caerphilly East Junction, can still be seen, a single track of rotted sleepers with their GWR-marked chairs still in position. This track winds its way for a short distance towards Machen; now overgrown with small bushes and weeds, it is another sharp reminder of better days now long gone. *Caerphilly Library*

Below This view of Caerphilly station was taken from the passenger overbridge, facing east, and shows once again pannier tank No 6411, returning from Newport with its auto-trailer leading, as it approaches the station platforms on 14 September 1956. *S. C. L. Phillips and D. K. Jones*

By the Machen Loop Act of 1887 the PC&N was authorised to double the Brecon & Merthyr's Caerphilly branch, and a new down line was laid on a diverging route from Gwaun-y-Bara Junction to Machen, with the former single line becoming the up line; this gave an easier gradient of 1 in 200 for loaded coal trains to climb, rather than the 1 in 39 that they had to face previously. This new up line was brought into use on 14 September 1891, and was then transferred to Brecon & Merthyr ownership. In return the B&M paid 50 per cent of the annual net earnings from its Caerphilly branch to the PC&N.

Above Gwern-y-Domen Halt, east of Caerphilly on the Brecon & Merthyr Railway was opened for passenger services in October 1908, and closed entirely on 17 September 1956. Seen here are the rather neglected remains of the Halt on 4 October 1957. Today all traces have vanished, with only a cleared area of trees and the roadbridge abutments marking the spot where the Halt stood and where the line passed as it made its way towards Gwaun-y-Bara Junction. *S. C. L. Phillips and D. K. Jones*

Left Fountain Bridge Halt was located on the PC&N's Machen Loop line and was served by down (Machen-bound) trains only. Opening for passenger services in October 1908, it also closed entirely on 17 September 1956. This photograph, taken from the road above this halt on 30 August 1956, gives a clear view of the Halt and river bridge, and shows a former GWR engine of the '51' Class, No 4130, pulling a Caerphilly to Newport train. Today this line is also very overgrown, the trackbed under the road bridge has become waterlogged, and the river bridge has long since been dismantled. *S. C. L. Phillips and D. K. Jones*

Above Waterloo Halt also opened in October 1908. Being situated on the original Brecon & Merthyr Machen Loop line, it was served by up trains only. This clear photograph, taken on 17 September 1950, gives a good view of the former GWR auto-trailer. The Halt closed with the others on 17 September 1956, and today the site is the garden of a bungalow; the embankment that carried the line can still be followed, but with difficulty. *V. C. Hardacre*

Below Former GWR '37' Class engine No 3714, built in 1936, is seen here with an auto-trailer approaching Waterloo Halt on 15 September 1956, two days before closure. *S. C. L. Phillips and D. K. Jones*

SPECIAL WHISTLES.   Main Lines (Con.)

STATIONS AND JUNCTIONS.	TO AND FROM	WHISTLES.	REMARKS.
Llantrisant Junction ...	Siding and No. 2 Up	1 crow and 2	
	Tin Works and No. 1 Down	1 crow	
	South Sidings and Branch	1 crow	
Treforest Barry	Forest Steel and No. 2 Up ...	1 crow and 2 short	See Special Instructions, pages 22 and 23.
	Warehouse and No. 1 Down ...	1 crow and 1 short	
	Barry Up and Down and vice versa ...	4 short	
	Barry Up Line Sidings... ...	1 crow	
Treforest North	Forest Steel Works Siding ...	4 short	
P. C. & N. Railway			See Appendix.
P. C. & N. Junction ...	Main Lines	3 and 1 crow	
	Bay Road and Branch	1 crow and 1 short	Down Main Line Trains will use the Standard Whistle for the road upon which they require to travel
35	„ and Down Line	1 crow and 2 short	

A tail lamp and swing iron must be kept at P.C. and N. Junction to be used by engines returning from Newport, and having to run light on No. 2 Down road to Treforest Barry for empties.

P. C. & N. and B. & M. RAILWAYS.

STATIONS AND JUNCTIONS.	TO AND FROM	WHISTLES.	REMARKS.
Interchange Siding ...	Up and Down Main Line	1	T.V.R. trains will carry 1 White at Chimney, 1 White on left Buffer from Pontypridd to Alexandra Dock.
	Up to Down and vice versa	1 and 2 short	
	Down Main and Full Siding nearest Main Line	1 and 1 short	
	Down Main and No. 2 Full Siding ...	2 short and 1	
	Up Main and Empty Sidings No. 1 ...	2 short	
	„ and „ No. 2 ...	2 and 2 short	
Quarry Siding	Main Line and Quarry	1 crow	
Penrhos Junction ...	Up and Down	2	
Caerphilly West ...	Up and Down	2	
Caerphilly East	Up and Down	2	
Machen Junction ...	Up and Down	2	Up and Down Main Lines 1 long.
75	Station Sidings	2 short and 1 crow.	

P. C. & N. and B. & M. RAILWAYS (Con.)

STATIONS AND JUNCTIONS.	TO AND FROM	WHISTLES.	REMARKS.
Machen Junction ...	Main Line	1	
	Caerphilly Branch	2	
	Station Sidings	2 short and 1 crow	
	South Sidings	2 short and 1 long	
	North Sidings	3 short	
	Cross over Road	2 crows	
Machen Shop Box ...	Main Line	1	
	Sidings West of Up Line	2 short	
	Locomotive Sidings West of Up Line ...	1 short and 1 crow	
	Compound Crossing Up to Down ...	3 short and 1 crow	
Machen Lime Kiln ...	Main Line	1	
	Coal Siding High Level	2	
	Lime Siding Low Level	3	
	Cross over Road	2 crows	

Extracts from the Taff Vale Railway Rule Book of 1894 showing special arrangements for operating PC&N trains over the B&M. *Courtesy D. G. Thomas*

An extract from the *Cardiff Times* of 3 January 1925. *Cardiff Public Library*

Train in Landslide.
FIVE WAGONS WRECKED NEAR MACHEN.

A train of empty wagons was travelling to the Rhondda Valley from Newport on Tuesday night, and when about 1½ miles from Machen Station a landslide was responsible for wrecking five of the wagons.

Fortunately the driver and fireman were able to maintain their posts and bring the rest of the train to a standstill.

This did not interfere with any of the passenger trains to any great extent, as all the traffic was worked over one road.

A former GWR pannier tank with the 4.58 pm Machen to Pontypridd auto-train approaching White Hart Halt on 29 August 1956. Opened for passenger services on 12 May 1947, the Halt was located on the down section of the PC&N Machen Loop line, so only down trains stopped here. Today the Halt is long gone, and the embankment that carried the line is now overgrown with brambles and wild roses, effectively hiding all traces. *S. C. L. Phillips and D. K. Jones*

A sketch of White Hart Halt showing pannier tank No 6411 waiting for passengers for the last time on the day of closure, 30 June 1952. No 6411 was one of the '64' Class engines, built at Swindon Works in 1934. *The late Mr A. Merchant*

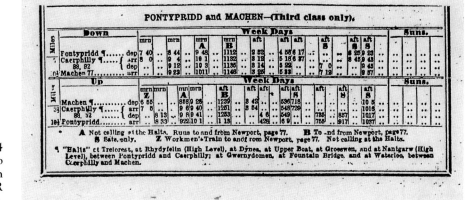

An extract from Bradshaw for July 1944 showing the service from Pontypridd to Machen and listing the Halts. The column headed 'A' shows the times of the GWR through service. *Courtesy of T. D. Chapman*

Above This view of these Machen looplines on 14 September 1956 gives a good indication of the steepness of the original line (on the left) and the lesser gradient of the new PC&N line. Approaching on the latter is former GWR '94' Class pannier tank No 8493, built in 1952 by Robert Stephenson & Hawthorns, with the 12.55 pm Caerphilly to Newport train. The line on the right is the former Brecon & Merthyr line to Machen via Trethomas. *S. C. L. Phillips and D. K. Jones*

Below This photograph, looking towards the junctions in the last year of the private pre-Grouping companies, June 1921, shows the B&M's Machen station with the PC&N service in the sidings. In the distance is the goods shed at Machen West Junction.

Today the trackbed is sadly overgrown with yellow-flowered gorse bushes and small saplings grow unchecked on both the up and down Loop lines that came together here; the junction is now fenced off and privately owned. *D. K. Jones*

A more elevated view of Machen station on 21 May 1955, again looking north-west towards Machen West Junction. Pannier tank No 6411 is seen again, shunting the auto-train from Caerphilly clear of the main line, on which a Newport to Brecon train is due. Thirty-four years earlier, in the previous photograph, this same movement would have been carried out to put the PC&N train into the sidings.

However, things were about to change. The Pontypridd to Machen passenger service continued to be operated by British Railways only until 17 September 1956, when it was withdrawn. No 6433, with two auto-coaches and carrying a wreath on its smoke-box door, made the final journey. *F. Hornby*

Above Machen station, looking in the opposite direction towards Church Road station. Ex-GWR engine No 351, formerly Taff Vale Railway Class 'A' No 91 built in 1921, is seen with auto-trailer No 103 attached, shunting between platforms to form the 7.25 pm train back to Caerphilly on 13 September 1951. *R. M. Casserley*

Below This photograph shows the completed movement, with No 351 at the front and the auto-trailer behind ready to form the 7.25 pm to Caerphilly. As it waits for passengers some young enthusiasts are asking question.

Machen station closed to passenger services on 31 December 1962, and finally closed entirely on 16 July 1964. Today it has the abandoned look of neglect. The station buildings are still standing, but gradually falling into disrepair; the wooden waiting room, GWR-inscribed station seat and bordered flower beds are only a memory now, a memory of a once busy and important station. *R. M. Casserley*

Extracts from the Taff Vale Railway Rule Book of 1894, relating to working between Machen and Newport. *Courtesy of D. C. Thomas*

P. C. & N. and B. & M. RAILWAYS (Con.)

STATIONS AND JUNCTIONS.	TO AND FROM	WHISTLES.	REMARKS.
Church Road	Main Line	1	
	Sidings	2	
	Cross over Road	3	
Rhiwderin	Main Line	1	
	Siding	2	
	Cross over Road	3	
Bassaleg North Box	Up and Down Main	1	
	Down Relief Line	2 and 2 short	
	Down Siding North of Box	3 short and 1 crow	
	New Siding for Up Empties	1 short and 1 crow	
	Cross over Road	1 short and 1 long	
	Up Main and Relief	2 crows	
	„ to Yard	1 and 3 short	
	Down Main to Yard	6 short	

77

P. C. & N. and B. & M. RAILWAYS (Con.)

STATIONS AND JUNCTIONS.	TO AND FROM	WHISTLES.	REMARKS.
Bassaleg Station Box	Down Relief to Main Line	2 crows and 2 short	
	Down Main to P. C. & N. Line	3	
	„ to Siding	1 and 1 short	
	Station Cross over	1 crow and 4 short	
	Cross over on Bridge	3 long and 1 crow	
	G.W.R.	2 long	
	No. 1 Siding close to Junction	1 and 1 crow	
	No. 2 Siding close to Junction	1 and 2 crows	
	No. 1 Siding South of Engine Shed	1 crow	
	No. 2 „ „ „	2 and 1 short and 1 crow	
	No. 3 „ „ „	1 and 2 short	
	Main Line and Coal Siding	6 short and 1 crow	
	Maesglas Weighing Line	6 long	
	Engine to take Water on Viaduct	3 crows	

78

P. C. & N. and B. & M. RAILWAYS (Con.)

STATIONS AND JUNCTIONS.	TO AND FROM	WHISTLES.	REMARKS.
Viaduct Box	Through Trains	1 and 1 short	
Mendalgyffe Junction	To and From Main Line	1	
	Up Line and Storage and vice versa	2	
	Down Line and Storage and vice versa	2 and 1 short	

NOTE.—Special Passenger and Excursion Trains to carry the same Head Marks or Lights as Regular Trains, according to destination.

NOTE.—All engines and trains, including engines and trains of Foreign Companies, working on the Main Line and the various Branches, not otherwise provided for, must carry—
By day, 1 lamp at foot of chimney.
By night, 1 white light in same position.

79

The dispute between the PC&N and GWR at Bassaleg is settled - an extract from the *Pontypridd Chronicle*, 2 August 1884. *Pontypridd Public Library*

PONTYPRIDD, CAERPHILLY AND NEWPORT RAILWAY.

The mineral traffic on this railway is being gradually developed. The dispute between the Great Western Railway Company and the Pontypridd and Caerphilly Railway Company has been, to a certain extent, settled in such a way as to enable traffic to be sent from the Rhondda Valley to Newport. The running powers of the new railway company do not permit of the Taff Vale engines passing over the Great Western system, although a working arrangement will in all probability be entered into shortly; but the Great Western Company do not object to convey the traffic themselves. The Taff Vale Railway Company convey the mineral trains to Bassaleg Junction, thence they are conveyed to the Alexandra Dock by the engines of the Great Western Railway Company, and these engines return the empty wagons to the place whence they were taken. Under this arrangement several mineral trains are now passing to and fro on the new railway daily.

Church Road was the next station along the Brecon & Merthyr line from Machen to Newport High Street station. It is seen here looking towards Rhiwderin circa 1910. The station closed entirely on 16 September 1957; the station building is now in private hands. *Courtesy of* The Railway Magazine, *1918*

Rhiwderin station, on towards Bassaleg, closed to passenger services on 1 March 1954, and to goods on 14 September 1959. It is also now in private ownership and much of its former character has been retained, thanks to the present owners.

The B&M's Bassaleg station, looking towards Newport circa 1910. A through PC&N Newport to Pontypridd service is approaching, operated by GWR staff; it has just crossed the bridge that spans the River Ebbw.

Bassaleg station closed to passenger services on 31 December 1962, and to goods traffic on 16 July 1964. Today the platforms are still in good condition, although the waiting room seen here has long gone, and a restaurant has been built on the site of the station buildings. *Lens of Sutton*

From Park Junction, 1 mile from East Mendalgief Junction, Newport, the double-tracked PC&N line ran parallel with the Western Valleys line of the former Monmouth Railway & Canal Company, along a stretch of track known as the 'Golden Mile'. It was this short stretch of line that became infamous due to the fact that all lines to the docks passed through Lord Tredegar's estates, and a levy of 1 penny per ton per mile was charged.

Park Junction opened in April 1886 for goods and mineral traffic, and closed on 28 November 1966. This view of the junction was taken during alteration of the layout to include up and down relief lines from the Park Junction to Gaer Tunnel. Date unknown, possibly 1910. *T. Jukes*

A more recent view of Park Junction, showing former GWR '56' Class 0-6-2T No 5697, built at Swindon in 1927, in British Railways livery with an up valleys freight on 11 March 1959. *S. Rickard*

A Brecon & Merthyr 0-6-0 saddle tank engine, one of the double-framed design, seen at Newport station. These sturdy engines were excellent machines, and could be seen working both passenger and goods trains. This example, No 31, is seen with a passenger train on the B&M's Newport to Rhymney service departing from this GWR station circa 1902. These engines were all withdrawn around 1920-21. *Courtesy of The Railway Magazine, 1913*

Platform 4 at Newport station, with an auto-train consisting of a GWR '57' Class pannier tank and Driving Brake 2nd coach No W247W waiting for passengers on 27 May 1956. *F. Hornby*

6.
LINES INTO THE DOCKS

PC&N

The line from Bassaleg to the sidings at Mendalgief opened in April 1886. From Bassaleg Junction to Bassaleg Loop, a distance of 6 chains, the line was single track, with the line north of Bassaleg Loop signal box to East Mendalgief Junction being double track, worked by the Tyers Absolute Block system. 'Permissive block' was installed from Bassaleg Junction to Park Junction during the latter part of 1938 because of the installation of crossovers for relief dock lines at Bassaleg Junction. Bassaleg Loop closed to traffic on 3 September 1959.

Beyond Park Junction the line crossed the South Wales main line from Newport to Cardiff by means of overbridges to reach West Mendalgief Junction, from there dropping down the embankment on which the signal box stood to reach Mendalgief East Junction, and from there into the North and South Docks internal lines (see the map on pages 24-5).

The track serving Lord Tredegar's Park Yard covered an area of 90 chains by 1 mile 37 chains, and was retained until their removal on 7 December 1967. It is fitting that the last piece of track from the PC&N line should come from the former estates of the late Lord Tredegar.

GWR

In 1880 the GWR took over the Monmouth Railway & Canal Company, and this company's traffic from the coalfields of the Western Valleys of Monmouthshire was conveyed towards the ANDR's North Dock, and later the South Dock, over the former MRCC lines. After the GWR took over these lines at the Grouping of 1922, the area was renamed as the Great Western Railway's Monmouthshire & Western Valleys Division.

From West Mendalgief Junction running powers were formerly granted by the GWR to the PC&N for its traffic to run on the former MRCC metals. This junction was

Maesglas Junction was opened on 10 April 1875, and was resignalled in 1896 due to the increased amount of traffic that was entering the Alexandra Docks from the GWR system at this point. This photograph shows the junction during an SLS railtour visit on 11 July 1959; it was eventually closed on 3 September 1979. *J. J. Davis*

rebuilt by the GWR on 3 February 1928, and closed on 20 May 1960.

The line from East Mendalgief Junction, where the ANDR and PC&N lines met, to the GWR's Alexandra Dock Junction on the South Wales main line was opened on 10 April 1875, with running powers granted to the PC&N. In 1896 this junction was resignalled, and became a common conveying point for the rail traffic entering or leaving the Alexandra Docks. A GWR memo dated 26 June 1930, issued from the Chief Dock Manager's Office, Cardiff, describes the situation: 'While the statu-

tory railway of the Alexandra Docks Company terminated at East Mendalgief Junction, between that point and ship's side the traffic had to be hauled for varying distances to and from the respective coal hoists and general cargo quays at the dock. . . Traffic to and from the Great Western Railway Company was exchanged either at Maesglas Junction or the Alexandra Dock Junction, with the Alexandra Docks Company working the traffic in either direction between these junctions and the ship's side.'

East Mendalgief Junction was closed to traffic on 20 November 1966.

Above This aerial view of circa 1937 shows the extensive railway network that led into the Alexandra Docks, and can be compared with the map on pages 24-5. 'A' (the white roofs in the middle distance) is the Whitehead Iron & Steel Works, over to the right is 'B', British Briquettes Limited, and next to them is 'C', the works of Messrs Braithwaite & Co (Engineers). In the middle is 'D', the top end of the North Dock, and over to the left is 'E', part of the Timber Float. *Newport County Council*

Right This aerial view gives a closer view of the Whitehead Court-y-Bella Works. To the left of the buildings is the extensive network of the Monmouthshire Bank Sidings. Circa 1937. *Author's collection*

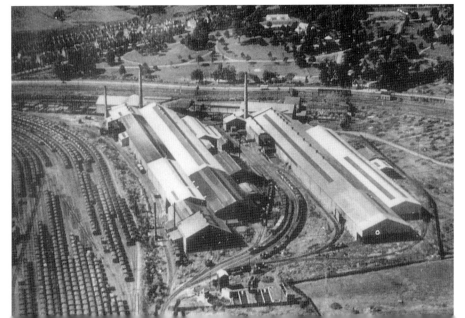

Above   This photograph, looking north-westwards from East Mendalgief Junction circa 1930, shows the sidings towards West Mendalgief on the left and the Monmouthshire Bank sidings on the right. The building on the extreme right might possibly be Monmouthshire Bank Cabin signal box. *Associated British Ports*

Left   A special train from the Brown, Lenox Works at Pontypridd entering the Alexandra Docks via the PC&N line in April 1934. The load, which consisted of Admiralty mooring buoys, was eventually shipped out of the docks on 22 April 1934 aboard the SS *Greyfriars* en route to Rosyth in Scotland. The buoys weighed 6 ton 18 cwt each, and measured 13 feet by 10 feet. They are seen here on GWR 'Crocodile B' bogie trolleys, which carried a load of 15 tons. *Associated British Ports*

Left   This photograph, circa 1910, shows the extensive use to which the Storage Sidings were put, and the tremendous amount of sidings needed to accommodate the vast number of private colliery coal wagons that were en route to the west side of the South Docks. *Associated British Ports*

Internal dock lines

The internal dock lines of the ANDR began at East Mendalgief Junction. The Alexandra Docks were at one time served by a continuous procession of wagons and coal trucks, with the sidings providing accommodation extending to upwards of 100 miles in length, and by 1914 covering a ground space of over 50 acres. Also provided free was storage space for the stacking of rails and iron ore for a period of 90 days prior to shipping, when required. By 1932 the storage and siding accommodation had been increased to hold 12,000 wagons.

The Tank Sidings were so called because they were adjacent to a sludge tank, into which the bilge contents of vessels were pumped. These sidings were removed some time in the 1970s. Cork Sidings were used for the storage of cattle, which had been shipped over from Ireland and disembarked at Cork Wharf. Again these were removed in the 1970s. Marshalling Sidings were formerly situated on the west side of North Dock, and were also lifted some time in the early part of the 1970s; they were also known as Storage Sidings.

As can be seen, although there was a complicated amount of junctions and sidings in the maze of lines in the Alexandra Docks complex, the distance between them was not great when compared with other railway companies - but they could be confusing when confronted for the first time!

Seen here are the tracks leading into the docks circa 1910. Those on the left lead to the west side of North Dock, while those going straight on lead to the coal hoists at South Dock. *ANDR booklet of 1916*

Rolling Bridge Junction, circa 1910. Originally the bridge was hydraulically operated and had a travel of 107 feet, the whole structure being carried on cast iron cylinders 8 feet in diameter with an average depth of 54 feet. A speed of 5 mph was imposed on all traffic crossing this bridge. After the extension of the track to the Salvage Factory in 1915 the bridge was fixed in position, its new name replacing the former one of Rolling Bridge Crossing. In 1934 the Salvage Factory became No 9 transit shed, and extra sidings were laid that same year to provide accommodation for an extra 671 railway wagons. The photograph shows the bridge from the south. *ANDR booklet of 1916*

Deal timber in transit from the ship to the timber yards inside Alexandra Docks circa 1910. *ANDR booklet of 1916*

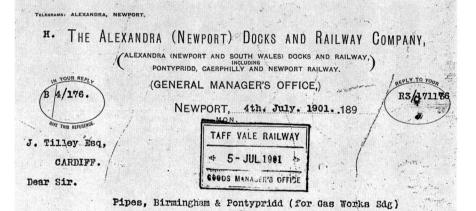

TELEGRAMS: ALEXANDRA, NEWPORT.

H. THE ALEXANDRA (NEWPORT) DOCKS AND RAILWAY COMPANY,

(ALEXANDRA (NEWPORT AND SOUTH WALES) DOCKS AND RAILWAY,
INCLUDING
PONTYPRIDD, CAERPHILLY AND NEWPORT RAILWAY.)

(GENERAL MANAGER'S OFFICE,)

NEWPORT, 4th. July. 1901...189

IN YOUR REPLY
B 4/176.
GIVE THIS REFERENCE.

REPLY TO YOUR
R3/171176

TAFF VALE RAILWAY
5 - JUL.1901
GOODS MANAGER'S OFFICE

J. Tilley Esq,
CARDIFF.

Dear Sir.

Pipes, Birmingham & Pontypridd (for Gas Works Sdg)
———o———

With reference to the copies of invoices sent with your letter of 14th May. The receipts on this traffic have not been included to this Company by R. C. H. and upon our Audit office taking up with your Mr Lewis they are informed that the entries have been included to your Company.

I shall be glad to know what steps your people took, when they discovered that the traffic had been dealt with wrongly by R. C. H, to put latter right for the future.

Have Clearing House got clear instructions respecting the inclusion of traffic for places on this Company's system.

Yours truly.

for John Macaulay.

A letter from the General Manager's Office, Newport Docks, dated 1901, and still showing the original ANDR title 20 years after it was changed to the longer title below. *D. Rees collection*

7.
LOCOMOTIVES AND ROLLING-STOCK

Steam railmotors

Railmotor No 1, which was built by the Glasgow Railway & Engineering Co Ltd, Govan, Glasgow, in 1904, and fitted with 3-foot disc wheels. This photograph shows ANDR Company staff and officials during the railmotor's acceptance trials of 1 September 1904, quite an important occasion. *Welsh Industrial & Maritime Museum, Cardiff*

An interior view of Railmotor No 1 circa 1904, showing the seating capacity for 52 passengers. The overall length of the rail-motor was 55 ft 6 ins, and this seating arrangement lasted until 1911, when it was rebuilt into an ordinary carriage with seating for 68 passengers.

After the Grouping the railmotor was renumbered as coach No 95. On 1 September 1928 it was transferred to service stock as loco workman's coach No 173, finally being withdrawn from service on 22 September 1934. *Associated British Ports*

Railcar No 2 of 1905, which was also built by Glasgow Railway & Engineering. It had an overall length of 61 ft 3 ins, and like No 1 was also rebuilt, to carry 58 passengers. On 1 September 1923 the GWR renumbered it as coach No 90, and it was finally withdrawn from service on 25 October 1930. This railcar had a clerestory roof, and is seen here at the Alexandra Docks after purchase in 1905. *Associated British Ports*

Steam locomotives

Most of the Alexandra Docks engines had short 0-6-0 or 0-4-0 wheelbases and were of the saddle or pannier design, which was essential for dock working, especially with the tight curvature of the internal lines presenting the ever-present danger of a derailment, which could not only cause serious injury but would also cause unwanted delay and loss of revenue.

Today the types of engines that work inside the docks are British Rail '08' Class diesel shunters, reliable workhorses in their own right.

Trojan, an 0-4-0 saddle tank engine, in use at the Alder Paper Mill at Tamworth. It was built in 1897 by the Avonside Engine Company to work with the other 0-4-0 engine *Alexandra* in the Town Dock. After the Grouping the GWR did not want these non-standard engines, so in July 1934 *Trojan* was withdrawn and sold to the Moira Colliery and then to the Victoria Colliery,

Wellington. Finally in December 1947 it was transferred to the Alder Paper Mills. Apart from the removal of the chimney cap, the substitution of a deeper-toned whistle and the extension of the cab side sheet, this engine was almost in its original condition when photographed with its GWR number 1340 on 22 April 1958. *R. M. Casserley*

ANDR 0-4-0 *Alexandra*, seen here with its GWR number 1341 at the former Taff Vale Railway's yard at Cathays, Cardiff, on 11 May 1927; by the look of the background scene, it is next to the Woodville Road bridge. *Alexandra* was built in 1884 by Hawthorn Leslie at their works at Newcastle-upon-Tyne. It was withdrawn from service in 1946 and cut up at Caerphilly engine shed in July of that year. *R. M. Casserley*

Seen here at Newport is ANDR engine No 1, photographed with its driver and fireman on 31 July 1905. It was an 0-6-0 saddle tank built by Robert Stephenson in 1898. Later it was renumbered by the GWR as 674, and was withdrawn from service in 1929. *LCGB (Ken Nunn Collection)*

ANDR No 3, another 0-6-0 saddle tank photographed at the Alexandra Docks on 31 July 1905. This engine was also built by Robert Stephenson, in 1900, renumbered by the GWR as 676, and finally withdrawn in 1929. *LCGB (Ken Nunn Collection)*

Above Engine No 7, named by the ANDR as *Pontypridd*, one of the company's coal train engines. Built by Sharpe in 1857, it was originally purchased by the London & North Western Railway (LNWR) and is seen here at Pontypridd in 1884. It was eventually withdrawn from service in 1900. *Welsh Industrial & Maritime Museum, Cardiff*

Below ANDR engine No 9, with attendant staff. This Beyer Peacock engine was built in 1887 and was one of those purchased by the ANDR in November/December 1903 from the former Mersey Railway Company. It was with this engine that the submerged coal trials and experiments were carried out (see opposite). Renumbered by the GWR as 1211, it was withdrawn in 1929. It is seen here just after delivery, probably in 1904. Syren and Shipping *magazine*

Experiments with submerged coal

Early this century an article by Lord Charles Beresford appeared in *The Times* newspaper, concerning the marked loss of calorific power in coal that was stored for naval use at coaling stations abroad, and thus the loss of power to the Royal Navy's vessels.

Shortly after reading this article ANDR General Manager Mr Macauley noted that the dredger at work alongside one of the coal hoists was bringing up an occasional lump of coal that had tumbled into the water during the course of shipping. He was struck with the idea that the storage of coal under water might enable the calorific value to be retained, perhaps better than when exposed to the air.

Enquiries were promptly set in hand as to the general quality of any coal that had been recovered from the ANDR docks. It was found that when any available quantity worth separating from the mud was recovered, it was used for minor purposes during the winter periods by the men working around the docks. To the amazement of some, far from having deteriorated it was found that this coal was better - it burned more cleanly, and gave a better flame.

One example was a small furnace that was kept burning day and night near the Alexandra Docks engine shed for the purpose of drying sand for locomotive use; occasionally a shovelful of live coals was used to assist in the making up of a locomotive fire after the cleaning-out process. A quantity of small dredged coal was from time to time burned and found to be particularly good.

To a certain extent comparison was practicable at this initial stage, for the sweepings around the hoists were also used at this furnace, and the coal that had been under water was found to be far superior, and was always greeted with joy by the stoker when available. In short, the coal that had been under water for some time was far superior to that mined within a week of being used, both being in the same physical state, ie 'small'.

The coal recovered from the dock had been under water for a period of between six to nine months. It had been impossible to dredge it sooner, and then only on Sundays unless absolutely necessary, owing to the great pressure of work during 1901-4, with the demand for hoists and the handling of coal shipments.

Mr Macauley was pleased with the results, as far as they went, but it was decided that they did not go far enough to enable a firm conclusion to be made. For instance, in the case of 'small' coal the improved results may have been due to the washing that the coal may have received, by which an amount of less valuable dust would have been washed away; on the other hand, a considerable proportion of the dredged coal could have been nothing more than dust, which, falling upon the surface of the water in the process of tipping had settled as sediment to the dock bottom.

The result of these findings and thoughts was that a series of tests were performed to get more accurate results, then they were again repeated even more carefully and elaborately. In the light of the experience gained a selected ANDR engine and crew were picked out for a series of practical experiments upon the company's railway between Pontypridd and Newport. The fullest records of the work carried out continuously on the footplate of the engine were carefully made and analysed, with every precaution taken to arrive at the correct result.

Laboratory experiments were able to confirm the practical tests, that coal known to have been submerged for periods ranging from one to three years would lose between 1 and 2 per cent of its calorific value, whereas coal exposed to air would lose from 10 to 12 per cent in this country, and in foreign stations having a higher temperature, especially if exposed to wind, probably nearly twice that amount. The lower loss with the submerged coal was held to be due to protection from oxidation by the enveloping water and the physical weathering effects of the sun, wind, rain and frost, and lastly by the more complete retention in the innumerable fissures of steam coal of its more volatile constituents, giving it a high burning value. It was also found that these results did not apply to any other type of coal other than Welsh; other varieties, being harder, lost far less through exposure to air.

The experiments had been carried out not to find a comparison between the keeping qualities of different coals, but to arrive at the best method of overcoming the pronounced tendency of Welsh coal - the best steam-raising coal in the world - to dissipate its energy upon exposure to the air. Welsh coal was a 'fuller' type and could hold the constituents necessary for producing power 'in the vein'; this conclusion was clear from the calorific degradation that commenced in the colliery itself, represented by the inflammable gases being given off, and against which many elaborate precautions had to be taken in the fiery seams of the South Wales coalfields.

Above ANDR engine No 12, seen here 31 July 1905 at the Alexandra Docks, was built by R. W. Hawthorn and sold to the ANDR in 1884. After the Grouping it was renumbered by the GWR as 664, and was withdrawn from the Alexandra Docks in 1930. By 1940 it had been sold to the Seaton Burn Colliery in the Northumberland coalfields, who renumbered it as SBC No 1. *LCGB (Ken Nunn Collection)*

Below ANDR No 13 with its crew circa 1884. This 0-6-0 saddle tank was also purchased from R. W. Hawthorn in 1884, and is seen here 'as new' at the Alexandra Docks. It was withdrawn in September 1926. *Welsh Industrial & Maritime Museum, Cardiff*

In 1917 the last of the two steam railmotors was withdrawn. As all coaches were now required to be loco-hauled, an extra engine was purchased to work the PC&N line. This was a former GWR 0-4-2T of the '517' Class, No 1426, which was renumbered 14 by the ANDR. This picturesque scene shows No 14 with its trailer coach picking up passengers at Groeswen circa 1917. *The Oakwood Press*

ANDR No 17, another 0-6-0 design, photographed at the Hawthorn Leslie Works at Newcastle-upon-Tyne on 29 April 1920. Renumbered 672 by the GWR, it did not last long with its new owners, being withdrawn in 1924. After withdrawal its boiler was rebuilt in 1927 and fitted to former ANDR engine No 16, which extended the latter's working life for a further ten years. *LCGB (Ken Nunn Collection)*

This view of former ANDR engine No 19 (right) shows it with its new GWR number 680 outside Oswestry shed next to GWR 2-4-0T No 617 on 31 May 1932. No 19 was built by Peckett & Sons in 1886, and after the Grouping, as No 680, it spent the rest of its life working from Oswestry shed. *R. M. Casserley*

Above ANDR 0-6-4T No 22 was purchased from the Mersey Railway Company, and is seen here at the Alexandra Docks on 5 August 1905. Note that it is still in Mersey Railway livery and has a painted on number. Built by Beyer Peacock in 1885, it did not last long after the Grouping; renumbered by the GWR as 1344, it was withdrawn in 1923.

Documents show that the heaviest coal trains were given to the company's three 0-6-4 tank engines, Nos 22, 23 and 24, with loads from Caerphilly and Bassaleg en route to the Alexandra Docks consisting of 70 wagons. *LCGB (Ken Nunn Collection)*

Below Seen here alongside other scrapped engines is ANDR 0-6-4T No 24, another of the Beyer Peacock engines of 1885, renumbered by the GWR as 1346 and withdrawn in 1927. It was photographed on the Swindon scrap lines on 11 September of that year. *R. M. Casserley*

Above ANDR 0-6-0 No 28 at the Alexandra Docks sidings circa 1909 (sometimes this photograph has been referred to as being at the Interchange Sidings, Pontypridd). No 28 was built at the GWR's Swindon Works in 1886, and remained in PC&N service for many years, being one of a pair of GWR '1661' Class engines purchased by the ANDR in 1906. After the Grouping it was renumbered 1683, and was finally withdrawn from service in 1926.

The two Barnum & Bailey coaches, sometimes referred to as

Pullman coaches, were purchased by the ANDR in 1909 (see page 113). *Pontypridd Public Library*

Below This 0-6-0 saddle tank was built by the GWR at its Wolverhampton Works in 1875 as No 993, and was purchased by the ANDR in 1913 and given the number 33. After the Grouping the GWR again renumbered it 993, and it was withdrawn in 1930. It is seen here in 1913 on one of the docks' numerous sidings. *Welsh Industrial & Maritime Museum, Cardiff*

Above 2-6-2T No 1205 passing Canton Sheds, Cardiff, on 10 September 1951. This Hawthorn Leslie engine of 1920 was one of the last built for the ANDR, who numbered it 36. A powerful 2-6-2 prairie tank, it could haul heavy coal trains yet was able to negotiate the sharp curves of the docks. Renumbered by the GWR as 1205, it was withdrawn from service in 1956. *R. M. Casserley*

Below Driver Reg Young and Fireman O'Shea in the cab of engine No 3714 pulling the last through train from Pontypridd to Newport, photographed here at platform 7 of Newport station at 08.35 am on 15 September 1956 (see also page 87). This GWR engine was built in 1936 and was allocated to Newport Ebbw Junction engine shed until withdrawal in 1963. *S. C. L. Phillips and D. K. Jones*

Pill engine sheds

The ANDR only had three engine sheds: one was at Glyntaff near to the goods depot there, the second was situated on the east side of the land that was lost when South Dock was excavated, and the third was at Pill, part of the docks complex.

Pill engine shed was opened by the ANDR in 1898, and was enlarged by the GWR to handle the extra engines that were transferred there when Newport Dock Street and Bassaleg engine sheds were closed. These closures were caused by the declining coal trade which brought with it the closure of the Town Dock and less traffic for the railways. The GWR also added extra coal-ing facilities in 1929. Access to this shed was gained via East Mendalgief Junction.

A feature of Pill was the grounded coach bodies used as mess rooms, offices and storeroom facilities. One of these was originally a fairly typical Edwardian non-corridor coach, but the other was of a type that most of us have only seen in Wild West films, described by the GWR as an American parlour car with 'end verandah'.

Pill was given the shed code 86B by British Railways in 1949. When the shed closed in June 1963 the engines allocated there were transferred to the nearby Ebbw Junction shed.

Right ANDR engine No 18, an 0-6-0 saddle tank, photographed outside Pill engine sheds on 31 July 1905. *LCGB (Ken Nunn Collection)*

Below Former Alexandra Docks engine No 16, rebuilt and renumbered by the GWR as 671, at Pill on 27 August 1931. This engine, withdrawn from service by the GWR in 1937, is hauling steel-bodied GWR coal wagons, possibly en route for engine shed use. *D. K. Jones*

Above No 666 at Pill shed on 4 May 1951. In the background can be seen one of the grounded coach bodies in use as a store or mess room. *R. M. Casserley*

Below GWR staff pose alongside Alexandra Dock shunting engine No 667 (GWR) circa 1927. This engine was formerly ANDR No 34, built at the Kerr Stuart Works in 1917, and was withdrawn from service by British Railways in 1954. In the cab are driver W. H. Walters and fireman Gregory; also in the photograph are Billie Davies, Joe Burgess and Ivor Harris. *Courtesy of Miss M. Parsons, granddaughter of the late W. H. Walters*

Barnum & Bailey coaches

After touring the United States for many years, in 1896 James Bailey of Barnum & Bailey's Circus decided to tour Great Britain; his partner for many years, Phineas T. Barnum, had died a few years earlier. Because of loading gauge restrictions imposed on their American-made carriages and rolling-stock, a contract was agreed with W. R. Renshaw & Company of the Phoenix Works, Stoke-on-Trent, to build the stock required for the tour.

Renshaw completed the initial contract for 68 assorted vehicles, and later others were to follow, based on the American design and painted in yellow with red lettering for the rolling-stock, and in dark lake with gold lettering for the passenger coaches. 'Barnum & Bailey, the Greatest Show on Earth' was ready to roll.

The first show was at Olympia, London, on 27 December 1897, and at the end of that season, on 12 November 1898, the circus had visited 72 towns. The second season began on 10 April 1899 and lasted until 11 November, visiting 112 towns before crossing the English Channel to Europe.

Colonel 'Buffalo Bill' Cody then hired 50 of these vehicles from Bailey and another tour was started; 'Buffalo Bill's Wild West Show' began on 26 December 1902, again at Olympia. By 1906 the tour was over and Cody returned to American, having toured not only Great Britain but also Europe.

The coaches and rolling stock were sold to Mr E. E. Cornforth of Trentham, Stoke-on-Trent, who disposed of 23 flat cars, two elephant cars and three passenger coaches to the ANDR in 1910. Two of the flat cars were fitted with British-type couplings at Renshaw's works to enable the movement of the complete batch of 28 vehicles from Stoke-on-Trent to the Alexandra Docks as one train. The passenger coaches retained their end balconies, but with the ANDR initials incorporated in wrought iron, while the underframe storage boxes were removed at Renshaw's before departure.

ANDR coach No 1, one of the former Barnum & Bailey Circus coaches purchased by the ANDR in 1910 for use on its Pontypridd, Caerphilly and Newport line, and seen after delivery. One of the first jobs that had to be carried out on these coaches was treatment for the removal of lice, an inheritance from their circus days.

Barnum & Bailey's Circus appeared at Cardiff on 21-24 June 1899, travelling on to Newport and opening there on 26 June, before moving onwards to Gloucester the next day. It is quite possible that members of the ANDR Board of Directors visited the circus and saw with interest the coaches and rolling-stock being used. It must have been quite an eye-opener in many ways!

The coach had a total length of 54 ft 6 ins. Its two four-wheeled bogies had a 7-foot wheelbase and were fitted with small 28-inch-diameter wheels; the floor was 11 inches lower than the British standard. *His Honour Judge Watkin Powell*

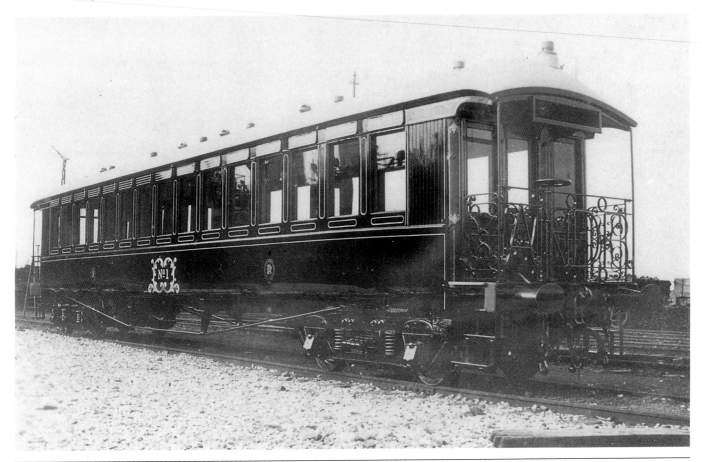

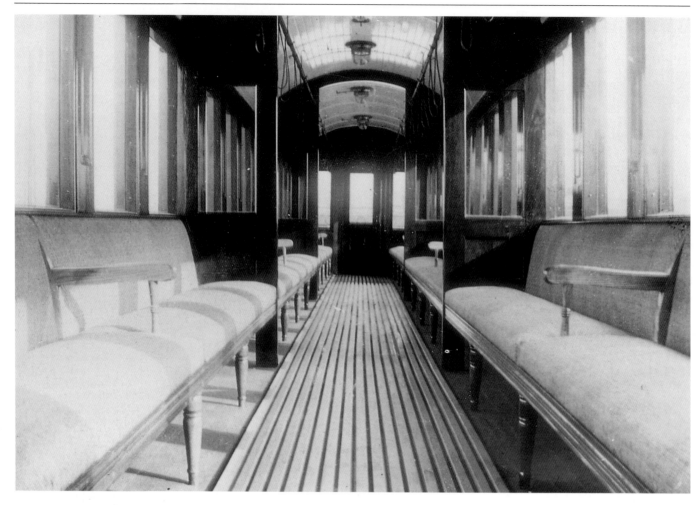

Above This interior view of ANDR coach No 1 in 1910 shows padded seats rather than the usual wooden slatted type of seating that would be used for 3rd Class accommodation by other railway companies.

One of the coaches was used as a stationary office at Pill engine sheds from 1920, and was officially withdrawn from service in 1923; the other two were taken out of service in 1926, one of them (possibly No 3) going into storage as condemned stock at Foss Cross on the former Midland & South Western Junction Railway. The other coach survived in departmental use with the GWR until 1934.

These two photographs are part of a collection that is on permanent loan from His Honour Judge Watkin Powell to the Welsh Industrial & Maritime Museum, Cardiff. *His Honour Judge Watkin Powell*

Left ANDR coach No 3, withdrawn by the GWR in 1926, awaiting restoration at the Welsh Industrial & Maritime Museum, Cardiff on 29 October 1988. It was discovered lying in a field in Devon, having been nearly broken up and burned by its former owner. Much work has still be to done, but given time this coach will resume its former character. *Author*

The elephant cars sold to the ANDR were numbered 104 and 105. This is No 105 with the British design of buffers and couplings seen at the left-hand end; the other end would have had the American buckeye type fitted. Elephant car No 104 would have had the wood-panelled sides reaching down to cover the well frame, almost to rail level, but as can be seen on No 105 it does not reach down so far. A common feature of these Barnum & Bailey vans was that the roof was rounded more than is usual, to meet the British loading gauge standards.

As with all the Barnum & Bailey circus vehicles, the floor of these elephant cars was built 11 inches lower than the British standard, and they had 7-foot-wheelbase bogies and small 28-inch-diameter wheels.

This photograph was taken at the Alexandra Docks, possibly on the day the vehicles were received, 2 September 1910. *Associated British Ports*

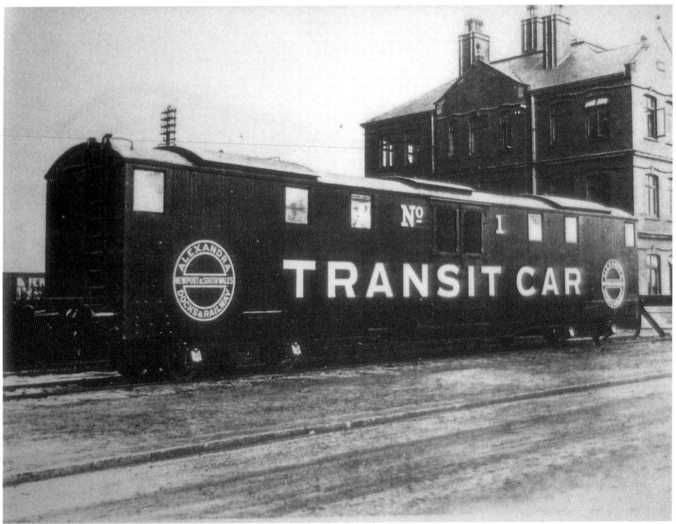

Elephant car No 105 rebuilt as ANDR Transit Car No 1 in September 1910, a miracle of reconstruction that took less than three weeks. *Associated British Ports*

8.
SIGNAL BOXES

Movement of the mineral traffic from the Rhondda and Cynon Valleys via Pontypridd station on to the PC&N lines en route to Newport Docks was controlled by PCN Junction signal box, situated at the southern end of Pontypridd station. This box closed in 1970 when the layout at Pontypridd station was simplified and colour light signalling installed; the former TVR Pontypridd Junction signal box took over all operations.

The line from PCN Junction to Penrhos Junction was double track and worked by Absolute Block. The first box along the line was Glyntaff, renamed Interchange Sidings East in 1906. The report of inspection by the Board of Trade dated 28 April 1906 states that the old PC&N Interchange Sidings signal box and the old connections with it are to be removed, and that the new Interchange Sidings signal box will contain 38 working and 12 spare levers, Glyntaff signal box containing 32 working and 10 spare levers. The new box was to be in use from 1 May 1906. At each of these signal boxes, which were on a very high embankment, some protective railing would be required at the side of the cabin to prevent accidents to the signalmen. By 9 April 1908 the new Interchange box contained 39 working levers and 3 spares. Groeswen signal box was 2 miles 63 chains from Glyntaff, and Penrhos Junction 1 mile 55 chains beyond there. Beyond Caerphilly, Gwaun-y-Bara Junction marked the beginning of the new PC&N Machen Loop for use by up trains, and opened on 14 September 1891; the new line passed Waterloo Halt and joined the main B&M line at Machen Junction, which was also known as Machen West Junction. Trains travelling down the other side of this loop passed White Hart Halt and Fountain Bridge Halt before crossing over the Rhymney River to reach Gwaun-y-bara Junction.

At Bassaleg, the station signal box was just 25 chains west of Bassaleg GWR Junction signal box; the latter was officially known as Bassaleg South signal box by 1907, but carried its former name until the 1950s. It closed on 10 May 1966. The PC&N's Bassaleg Junction signal box

was built circa 1900 and closed on 8 December 1968 when the junction becoming disused.

Glyntaff signal box, later renamed Interchange Sidings East, in 1904. *D. K. Jones*

Bassaleg Loop signal box closed on 16 August 1925, its function being taken over by Bassaleg Junction with the remodelling of the junction.

At Park Junction, the old GWR signal box (1 mile 14 chains from Bassaleg GWR signal box), which was built in 1882, was replaced by a larger box of GWR design on the same site. This box took over the function of Park Siding signal box, which closed in 1924. The new Park Junction signal box contained more than 100 levers to control the redesigned and enlarged juction layout. Forty-five chains further on was West Mendalgief Junction signal box; the original box was closed and replaced by a larger one of GWR design on the same site on 3 February 1928, and closed on 20 May 1960.

Maesglas Bank signal box opened in 1923, but it is believed to have closed on 3 February 1928.

East Mendalgief Junction signal box was originally built by the GWR in 1926 and contained 90 levers and McKenzie & Holland signalling equipment. During the Second World War brickwork was added for blast protection against German high-explosive bombs. This signal box closed in October 1976.

Maesglas ground frame was situated approximately 100 yards from Maesglas Junction signal box; it was taken out of use on 29 March 1927 but was retained for use by sig-

nalmen directing traffic into the docks area, becoming known as Monmouthshire Bank Cabin. Maesglas Junction signal box closed in 1968.

Monmouthshire Bank signal cabin, built in 1910 of McKenzie & Holland design, was situated 608 yards from Maesglas Junction signal box. This cabin could possibly have been the former Middle Connection signal box, but certainly was not the former Monmouthshire Bank Cabin of 1927. It closed in the 1960s, a period when the coal exports from the docks finally ceased and many of the sidings were gradually taken out of use.

Courtybella Junction signal box closed in October 1964, and Pill Bank Junction in November 1965.

Inside the docks Marshalling Sidings Ground Frame was situated at the junction of the lines leading to the west side of North Dock and those running behind the Timber Floats to serve coal hoists numbers 18, 19 and 20 in South Dock.

Rolling Bridge signal box, located on the north side of the bridge across the original South Lock, later renamed East Lock, opened in 1909. The movement of the bridge was interlocked with the railway signals and road barriers on both sides of the bridge. The box also contained the levers that lifted the bridge (which incidently reached a height of 4 ft 2½ inches, with a weight to be lifted of 450 tons). The time taken to lift the bridge was 1 minute.

Groeswen signal box, with members of the permanent way gang in attendance, in 1900. On the extreme left can be seen a cross carved into the embankment; possibly in remembrance of the death of a colleague or a beloved pet, it remains a mystery, the answer hidden by time. The box closed in 1956. *Pontypridd Public Library*

Above left Gwaun-y-Bara Junction signal box as it looked in the 1950s. It closed on 26 March 1956 and today little is left to show where the signal box or track was; only a slight rise of grass-covered earth and an occasional glimpse of ballast gives away its position. *Courtesy of the late T. B. Sands*

Left Maesglas Junction signal box, photographed during an SLS railtour visit to the Alexandra Docks complex on 11 July 1959. *J. J. Davis*

Above The approach roads to the Rolling Bridge, or East Lock Bridge, seen from the north. On the right of the bridge can be seen Rolling Bridge signal box. *Associated British Ports*

Right Park Junction signal box photographed in August 1988. This GWR-built box controlled the immense volume of traffic that used Newport Docks via Pye Junction and Park Junction. Today only two lines are used. *Author*

9.
STAFF AND MANAGEMENT

Below On 28 May 1868 Lady Tredegar performed the ceremony of the cutting of the first sod that officially started the excavation of the Alexandra North Dock, under the expert guidance of engineer-in-charge Mr Abernethy. The dock was opened on 13 April 1875, but the public rejoicing was greatly marred by the serious illness of the Chairman, the first Lord Tredegar, whose chair was kept vacant throughout the banquet and celebrations. He died on the 16th, and was succeeded by his son, the Honourable Godfrey Charles Morgan (pictured here in about 1900).

Sir Godfrey was born at Ruperra Castle in 1831. He served with the 17th Lancers during the Crimean War, attaining the rank of Captain, and was one of the few survivors from the 'Charge of the Light Brigade' at Balaclava. Years later when his gallant steed Sir Briggs died it was buried in the grounds of Tredegar House,

Newport, along with his Skye terrier Peeps. From 1858 until 1875 Sir Godfrey was a Member of Parliament, serving as the elected Conservative member for Brecknockshire. When he became Lord Tredegar in 1875 he inherited estates in Brecknockshire, Glamorganshire and Monmouthshire, a total of over 40,000 acres. He became Colonel of the Monmouth Engineer Militia in 1885, as well as patron for the University College of South Wales and Monmouthshire. He died on 11 March 1913.

The board of the ANDR, of which the second Lord Tredegar was Chairman with 60 shares, also included Sir George Elliot (50 shares), Mr Frank McClean (50), Mr E. M. Underdown (10), Mr G. W. Elliot (10) and Mr J. C. Parkinson (10). The other shareholders were Mr G. P. Bidder (10), Mr Robert Griffin (five), Mr Charles Rose (five), Mr Abernethy (one), Mr Carlisle (one), Mr Markby (one), and Mr Burt (one). Syren and Shipping *magazine*

Above right Mr John Macaulay was the General Manager of the ANDR from 1901 until 1 May 1913. He was born in Edinburgh in 1853 and entered the service of the North British Railway in 1866, at the age of only 13. In 1874 he transferred to the Cheshire Lines Committee, and subsequently became Superintendent at the Brunswick Dock station, Liverpool, remaining there for ten years. In 1894 he became Traffic Manager of the Mersey Tunnel Railway, and during his first six years he increased that company's profits by £6,000 per year. He also introduced and pioneered the use of electrification on that line. During his career he held posts as a Justice of the Peace for Monmouthshire, became a member and Chairman of the Newport Harbour & Pilotage Commissioners, and an associate of the Institute of Civil Engineers, as well as being appointed to a seat on the Board of the former Mold & Denbigh Railway Company.

Mr Macaulay was also an author. His work entitled *Modern Railway Works*, published in 1912, was a very descriptive engineering book.

Mr Macauley's Personal Clerk was Frank Brown, who had entered the service of the London & North Western Railway at Euston in 1896, where he undertook five years of station and traffic work before leaving to join the ANDR. In 1903 he became Parliamentary and Staff Clerk to the General Manager, and in 1908 organised the Company Staff Department and became the Secretary for the ANDR's side on Conciliation Boards.

In March 1916 he became assistant to the General Manager of the ANDR, Mr J. H. Vickery; on the amalgamation with the GWR at the Grouping, the latter was appointed Chief Docks Manager, with Mr Brown as his Assistant. Syren and Shipping *magazine*

Below left J. H. Vickery. In *The Railway Magazine* of 1922 a short article appeared on Mr Vickery, quoted here with the permission of the editor:

'Mr John Herbert Vickery was the General Manager of the ANDR Company at the time of amalgamation into the Great Western Railway, and was offered a new position as the Chief Docks Manager for the GWR Company, his headquarters becoming the Pierhead Building at Bute Docks, Cardiff.

'Mr Vickery gained his experience during the course of a varied career with the London & South Western Railway, beginning as a junior clerk in the goods department and serving therein for eight years in various capacities, later becoming Chief Clerk on the LSWR, in succession to Sir Sam Fay, and for many years acted as the Honourable Secretary to the London & South Western Railway Servants Orphanage, and Vice President of the LSW Railway Servants Temperance Union.

'In March 1913 he was selected to succeed Mr John Macaulay as the General Manager of the ANDR. As well as his railway duties he was also a Magistrate, President of the Newport Development Association and Chairman of the Bristol Channel Dockowners Association.' *Courtesy of The Railway Magazine (1913)*

Below An illuminated memorial presented to J. H. Vickery on behalf of various bodies connected with Newport Docks congratulating him on his appointment to the post of Chief Docks Manager of the GWR. *Associated British Ports*

The Chairman and Board of Directors of the ANDR from 17 June 1914 until 18 June 1919. In the centre on the right is Stanley Baldwin MP, who died in 1947 after a long and honourable career in politics, holding the post of Prime Minister three times. *Associated British Ports*

Members of the ANDR's police force, circa 1916. *Associated British Ports*

The ANDR's lock gate staff at East Lock, circa 1914. *Associated British Ports*

A very faded photograph of the ANDR Docks Strike Committee, circa 1911-12. Back row, left to right: C. Lawrence, R. Roberts, J. Fennesey, J. Landers. Third row: W. J. Baker, J. Collins, J. Murray, M. Hardy, C. Dyer, J. Kiley, M. Lynch, D. Driscoll, J. Morgan. Second row: W. Jones, J. O'Brien, A. Gould, C. Evans, J. Barber, F. Broad, P. Knight, G. Lovatt, A. Collins. Front row: J. Lynch, J. McAuley, J. K. Price, J. O'Leary, A. J. Kenny, J. Cadogan, G. Jackson, H. Seer, T. Sunday, F. Woolen, J. Bragg.

Just visible above them is the motto of the Strike Committee, taken from the Bible (Ecclesiastes, Chapter 9, Verse 10): 'Whatsoever thy hand findeth to do, do it with thy might.' *Courtesy of Starling Press Publishers*

The ANDR rugby team, photographed on 30 April 1920 after beating the Town Hall staff by one try, which was scored by M. Trew. Back row, left to right: A. J. Coles, S. B. Macay, A. Thomas, W. R. Jones, H. J. Williams, H. Smith, H. J. Gray, T. J. B. Cole, T. W. Mitchell, W. H. Victory, W. Sweet (linesman). Middle row: I. H. Gray, M. Trow, C. Channing, G. F. Jones, R. Dixon (Captain), H. R. Parfitt, L. Taylor, W. J. Martin (referee). Front row: W. Coakham, H. Edmunds, W. Lewis. *Associated British Ports*

The Alexandra (Newport & South Wales) Docks & Railway Company amalgamated with the Great Western Railway Company, Docks Department, on 25 March 1922. The company handed over 39 engines, 652 open goods wagons, nine brake-vans, six covered goods vans and 32 special wagons.

The GWR became part of British Railways upon nationalisation in 1948, and its Docks Department was passed on to the Docks & Inland Waterways Board, which in 1982 formed part of the Associated British Ports group.

This group photograph was taken outside the South Lock Power Station and shows the managerial staff of the ANDR at the time of the take-over by the GWR at the Grouping of 1922. *Courtesy of the late Arthur Wallis*

APPENDIX 1. PRESERVATION

The former ANDR coach No 3 can now be seen at the Welsh Industrial & Maritime Museum, at Butetown, Cardiff, South Glamorgan. Originally built for the Barnum & Bailey Circus to a standard American design, and later used by Buffalo Bill Cody's Wild West Show, it toured all over Great Britain and Europe. Together with other items of rolling-stock the coach was purchased by the ANDR in 1910 for use on its Pontypridd, Caerphilly and Newport line as part of its railmotor trailer sets. It was transported to the museum in December 1985 from its last resting place near Totnes in Devon.

The ANDR locomotive *Trojan*, currently owned by Mr John B. True can be seen at the Great Western Society, Didcot Railway Centre, Didcot, Oxfordshire. It is gradually being restored; much has been done so far, with new buffers of Avonside design fitted, a rolling chassis on order, and hopefully a new boiler to be fitted some time in the future.

Below ANDR coach No 3 awaiting restoration at the Welsh Industrial & Maritime Museum, Cardiff, on 29 October 1988. *Author*

Below right Tredegar House and Country Park, Newport, Gwent, the home of the Lords Tredegar from 1402 until 1962. It was taken over by Newport Borough Council in 1974, and has since been refurbished and much restored. Visitors will find the grounds, craft workshops, barns, mill, sunken garden, orangery, and tours of the house itself fascinating, with much on show regarding the history of this famous and respected family. The stable courtyard has recently undergone restoration and this will do much to add to the ornate splendour of the house. *Author*

APPENDIX 2.
ORDNANCE SURVEY MAP
REFERENCE NUMBERS

A present-day listing of all traceable halts, stations, sidings and junctions on the PC&N, Rhymney, Brecon & Merthyr and GWR lines into Newport's Alexandra Docks, with their respective Ordnance Survey map references.

PC&N line

PCN Junction, Pontypridd	ST072898
Broadway railway bridge, Pontypridd	ST073898
Tram Road Halt	ST073898
PC&N viaduct over River Taff	ST074898
Brown, Lenox works siding	ST076898 to ST079900
Interchange Sidings, West Junction	ST078898
Interchange Sidings, East Junction	ST084896
Glyntaff goods depot	ST085896
Glyntaff Halt	ST084896
Treforest Halt	ST086894
Cemetery Road bridge	ST086893
Glyntaff Gasworks Siding	ST089890
`High Level' Rhydyfelin Halt	ST091888
`GWR' Rhydyfelin Halt	ST093886
Dynea Halt	ST098883
Upper Boat Halt	ST108875
Groeswen Halt	ST115868
Railway bridge over track	ST118863
Railway bridge over stream	ST123861
Nantgarw Halt	ST124858
Nantgarw cattle creep	ST127857
Nantgarw roadbridge	ST128857

Rhymney Railway

Penrhos Junction	ST130857
Barry Railway viaduct abutments	ST136860
Penrhos South Junction	ST139862
Beddau North Junction	ST144863
Caerphilly, Watford Crossing	ST148864
Caerphilly, West Junction	ST153866
Caerphilly station	ST157865
Caerphilly East Junction (with B&M line)	ST161865

Brecon & Merthyr Railway

Caerphilly East Junction	ST161865
Caerphilly Van Road railway bridge	ST163867
Gwern-y-Domen Halt	ST177879
Gwaun-y-Bara Junction	ST179879
Viaduct over River Rhymney (site of)	ST190885
Fountain Bridge Halt	ST191885
Newport Road railway bridge	ST191885
Waterloo Halt	ST195883
Viaduct over River Rhymney	ST201888 to ST202889
Viaduct crossing river at	ST203889
White Hart Halt	ST205891
Up line railway bridge, Machen	ST210893
Down line railway bridge, Machen	ST210893
Machen West Junction	ST211893
Machen station and goods yard	ST211894
Machen Locomotive Works (site of)	ST217892
Church Road station	ST230883
Lower Machen railway bridge over A468	ST236878
Rhiwderin station	ST260874
Railway bridge near Rhiwderin station	ST260874
Bassaleg station	ST277872
Viaduct over River Ebbw near Bassaleg station	ST278872
Railway bridge over A467	ST282872

Great Western Railway

Bassaleg Junction, GWR	ST285868
Park Junction, GWR	ST296863
Park Mile, traceable from	ST286867 to ST294862
Gaer Tunnel (Park Junction end)	ST299866 to ST302868
Monmouthsire Bank Sidings	ST304868 to ST309864
West Mendalgief Junction	ST305864
Maesglas Junction (High Level)	ST303868
Alexandra Dock Junction	ST302867
Gaer Tunnel (Newport station end)	ST304873 to ST306879
Newport High Street station	ST309883

ANDR internal dock lines and locks				
East Mendalgief Junction	ST300864	North Lock (site of)	ST319856 to ST318855
Marshalling Sidings	ST311859 to ST316851	North Lock	ST314860 to ST310854
Middle Connection (Junction Cut)	ST318853	Baileys Dry Dock	ST320854 to ST318854
Rolling Bridge Junction	ST323852	1st South Lock	
ANDR Company headquarters	ST319856	(later East Lock)	ST322851 to ST323852
Pill engine shed	ST312862	2nd South Lock	
Timber Float (site of)	ST311855 to ST314851	(present entrance)	ST316843 to ST317837
		South Dock	ST318853 to ST325849 to ST314842

INDEX